Here's what they say about the *Knowledge in a Nutshell* books

"There are so many fascinating facts and stories in *Knowledge in a Nutshell*." –Dan Patrick, KSEV, Houston, Texas

"Fun stuff. Concise stories. There's something interesting on every page." —Spencer Hughes, KFBK, Sacramento, Calif.

"Not only are these books fun, but we learn a lot, too." —Jordan Rich, WBZ, Boston, Mass.

"The nuggets of information are like so many peanuts...you pick up one and you can't stop until these books are finished." —Michelle Pilicki, Pittsburgh Magazine.

Knowledge in a Nutshell

on the MOVIES

Charles Reichblum
Les Zittrain

arpr, inc

Paperbacks

Knowledge in a Nutshell on the Movies is the 6th book in the *Knowledge in a Nutshell®* series. The others: *Knowledge in a Nutshell, Knowledge in a Nutshell on Sports, Knowledge in a Nutshell on Popular Products—Heinz Edition, Knowledge in a Nutshell on America* and *Knowledge in a Nutshell on Success*. **Call** 1-800-NUTSHELL (1-800-688-7435) or visit www.knowledgeinanutshell.com.

KNOWLEDGE IN A NUTSHELL ON THE MOVIES

Copyright © 2003 by Charles Reichblum and Les Zittrain

ISBN: 0-9660991-2-5
Library of Congress Control Number: 2003094196

Printed in the United States of America, July 2003

Table of Contents

Dedication

This book for movie lovers everywhere is dedicated to our co-author, Les Zittrain who contributed mightily with his wit and wisdom (and love of movies) to the stories you'll be reading.

Sadly, before this book reached publication, Les died on January 26, 2003, at age 71, leaving behind a life full of service to his country, charity to his community, high ethical standards in his profession—and knowledge of his photographic memory of the film industry.

You could mention almost any movie ever made, and Les could tell you not only a story about it, but who was in it and even who directed it. Mention a movie star, and Les would have a fascinating morsel about that actor or actress.

That always surprised me because in Les' real (not reel) life, he was a prominent and respected lawyer in Pittsburgh and represented such sports stars as Pistol Pete Maravich, Terry Bradshaw, Joe Greene and Rocky Bleier, among others.

Movies, of course, were only one of Les' infatuations. The others were the love of his wife of 45 years, Ruth, who was also his law partner; his children Laura, Jeffrey and Jonathan; his grandchildren Rebecca, Hannah and Benjamin; the law itself; history; gardening; golf, tennis and fishing.

When I wrote my first "Knowledge in a Nutshell" book, Les read it cover-to-cover and called to say, "You know, it's very good, but you could have included this or that information in different stories." It was then that I decided to ask Les to be co-author if I ever did a book on the movies—and his many contributions are here to enjoy.

This book is a fitting tribute to the living memory of a great and good man, Les Zittrain.

A special "Oscar" goes to Les' wife Ruth. She helped tremendously in getting this book into its final form for all you movie buffs out there.

And the book is dedicated, as always, to my wife Audrey, our children Bob, Diane, Bill and Amalie, and our grandchildren Rachel, Justin, Noah and Clarissa for their inspiration.

Charles Reichblum

Special thanks to ⬛ Small at Advantar for the cover design and computer input.

ONE

Lights...Camera...Action

Why the Wizard was from Oz,
and other stories behind the stories

Why the Wizard
was from Oz

When Frank Baum wrote the original story of "The Wizard of Oz," he had settled on the word "Wizard" for part of his title, but was agonizing about what to call the place where the Wizard was from.

Taking a break from his writing one day, Baum gazed around his office. His eyes fell on the letters of three file drawers across the room.

One file read A-G. The next, H-N. The last, O-Z.

And "Oz" it became.

Surprising fact about
"The Wizard of Oz"

As great as Judy Garland was in the movie, she wasn't the first choice. MGM, which produced the film, wanted Shirley Temple for the lead. But 20th Century-Fox wouldn't release Shirley from her contract with them, so MGM settled for Judy.

An amazing oddity about "Casablanca"

When you first saw "Casablanca," the all-time favorite movie for many people, the interest kept building as to whether Humphrey Bogart and Ingrid Bergman would stay together, or go their separate ways, at the film's end.

The funny thing is that while the movie was being made, NEITHER THE ACTORS, NOR THE WRITERS, NOR THE DIRECTOR, knew how the story would end.

The three writers, Julius and Philip Epstein and Howard Koch, and the director, Michael Curtiz, couldn't make up their minds.

During the shooting of the movie, they decided to write two endings, one where Bogart and Bergman end up together, and the other where Bogart sacrifices his love to send Bergman off with Paul Henreid.

Finally they shot the second alternative first. They all liked it so much they never bothered to film the other version. And, as they say, that's the end of the story.

An incredible story about the Titanic

Six movies have been made about the famous sinking of the luxury liner Titanic, with the most popular being the 1997 Oscar-winning film starring Leonardo DiCaprio and Kate Winslet.

But here's a little-known, fascinating story about the Titanic.

Fourteen years BEFORE the real-life Titanic sank, a man named Morgan Robertson wrote a fiction book about a ship he named the "Titan."

In his book, Robertson's Titan was on its maiden voyage. It was said to be unsinkable. It was sailing from England to the U.S. It hit an iceberg. It sank in the North Atlantic. The time of year was mid-April.

ALL THOSE THINGS Roberston described in his book came true with the real Titanic. Robertson wrote his book in 1898. The real Titanic sank in 1912.

The toughest role to cast

More than 60 actresses took screen tests for the role of Scarlett O'Hara in "Gone With the Wind"—and none satisfied producer David O. Selznick.

He spent over $100,000 and used over 150,000 feet of film in his nationwide, publicity-driven search for the right person to play Scarlett.

Finally, with production ready to start, Selznick selected four women to take a final test—Joan Bennett, Jean Arthur, Paulette Goddard—and the most unlikely choice of all, Vivien Leigh. The part called for a southern accent, and Leigh not only had no southern accent, but she was British.

Selznick gambled, and surprised Hollywood, by picking Leigh for one of the most famous parts in movie history.

The gamble paid off. Leigh won the Oscar for Best Actress for her Scarlett.

Three suprises about "Gone With the Wind"

When Margaret Mitchell wrote "Gone With the Wind," she gave it a different name. She called it "Tomorrow Is Another Day."

But her publisher changed the title.

He wanted to convey the message that ways of life in the Old South were "gone with the wind."

The publisher also changed the heroine's first name.

Mitchell had chosen Pansy. The publisher made it Scarlett, to denote her fire.

Many people believe the last line in the book and movie was Rhett's famous "Frankly, my dear, I don't give a damn," but that is not true.

Scarlett, always determined to fight back, has the last words, saying, "After all, tomorrow is another day."

One last note on Margaret Mitchell: Her life ended prematurely. She was crossing a downtown street in Atlanta in 1949 when she was hit and killed by an automobile.

She was just 49.

"GWTW's" competition

When "Gone With the Wind" was first released in 1939, it had strong competition for the Best Picture Oscar.

1939 was a very good year for films—maybe the best in Hollywood history.

And in those days the Academy Awards nominated more movies for Best Picture than they do now.

Ten films were nominated that year: "Dark Victory," "Goodbye, Mr. Chips," "Gone With the Wind," "Love Affair," "Mr. Smith Goes to Washington," "Ninotchka," "Of Mice and Men," "Stagecoach," "The Wizard of Oz" and "Wuthering Heights."

And the winner was..."Gone With the Wind."

How the tradition started of Hitchcock appearing in the movies he directed

When Alfred Hitchcock directed one of his early movies, "The Lodger," in 1926, there was a scene where he needed one more extra. No additional extras were immediately available, so Hitchcock put himself in the momentary scene.

Because the film was a success, Hitchcock developed a superstition that he should appear briefly in all the movies he directed, and it became one of his trademarks.

However, later in his career, he felt it had become a distraction because moviegoers would try to spot him, and lose concentration on his story and effects. So, he tried to appear early in a film to get that over with.

Hitchock's biggest challenge was getting himself in his famous "Lifeboat." That movie holds the record for the smallest set ever employed in virtually an entire feature film, with all the actors confined to the lifeboat.

Hitchcock couldn't suddenly appear in the boat—but he solved it by having one of the actors hold up a newspaper. On the back page was an ad with Hitchcock's picture.

25-year-old man shakes up Hollywood

Orson Welles was only 25 years old when he produced, directed, co-wrote and starred in the film rated No. 1 of all time by the American Film Institute, "Citizen Kane."

Hollywood didn't know what to make of this man who had never directed or acted in a major film before "Citizen Kane."

He was considered an arrogant, unpopular, rank outsider. That probably played a big part in film insiders denying him an Oscar for Best Actor or Best Director for his classic work in "Citizen Kane."

Actually, Welles had shaken up much of America three years earlier with his network radio show, "The War of the Worlds," broadcast on Halloween Eve, 1938.

That program described a fictional invasion of the United States by Martians. Despite several disclaimers in the show that the invasion really wasn't happening, thousands of Americans panicked, jamming telephone lines, calling police, and running into the streets in terror.

Using real-sounding news bulletins, the program reported strange-looking beings from Mars shooting ray guns to kill everyone in sight. One woman in Pittsburgh was reportedly ready to drink a glass of poison until her husband stopped her.

Finally, at the end of the show Welles said it was all just a Halloween joke, and calm was restored. But Welles' celebrity was just starting.

How many times have you seen your favorite movie?

No matter how often you've watched a film that you liked, you probably haven't come close to Myra Franklin.

According to the Guinness Book of World Records, Ms. Franklin holds the record.

She has seen "The Sound of Music" 940 times.

The 1998 film that achieved the almost-impossible

Roberto Benigni starred in, co-wrote and directed one of the most unusual movies ever made, "Life is Beautiful."

It was about an Italian Jew thrown into a World War II concentration camp with his young son.

One critic wrote that Benigni achieved a feat "damn near unparalleled"—overriding the pathos of the situation with humor—as Benigni tries to fool his son that even in a concentration camp "life is beautiful" by turning their plight into a game.

Another critic said Benigni did the "almost impossible in pulling off this movie."

Benigni won the Best Actor Oscar for the film—and then was a sensation at the Academy Awards ceremonies.

When his name was announced as the winner, he jumped up and down on seats, and gave one of the most joyful acceptance speeches ever, alluding to the triumph of the human spirit in the movie.

One of the funniest lines
of all time

You could have a lot of enjoyment trying to recall the funniest lines ever said in a movie. In a recent, informal survey, the following is picked as No. 1, although this was a limited survey and you might want to name others as the funniest.

The choice here is from the 1989 film, "When Harry Met Sally."

Billy Crystal and Meg Ryan are sitting across from each other having lunch in a restaurant.

While they're talking, Ryan goes through all kinds of sexual gyrations and seems to be enjoying herself immensely.

A waitress approaches an older woman at the next table and asks her for her order. The woman looks at Ryan and says:

"I'll have what she's having."

(The person playing the older woman was Estelle Reiner, the mother of the picture's director, Rob Reiner).

Fact follows fiction

On March 16, 1979, a movie called "The China Syndrome," starring Jane Fonda, Jack Lemmon and Michael Douglas opened. It was a fictional thriller about an accident at a nuclear power plant.

Ironically, just 12 days AFTER the movie opened, the real thing happened. The most famous nuclear accident in U.S. history, with a partial meltdown of radioactive material, occurred at Three Mile Island, Pa.

Jack Lemmon couldn't believe it. He was quoted as saying, "Every goddamned thing we had in there came true."

The name of the movie, "The China Syndrome," comes from the phrase used by nuclear workers. It refers to the possibility of nuclear materials melting "all the way down to China" after a reactor goes bad.

The great car chase scenes

In a chase scene described by many critics as the best in movie history, Gene Hackman provides the action in 1971's "The French Connection."

Hackman drives a car at top speed in New York City under a train that's running above him on elevated tracks.

Hackman is chasing the train that holds a man he's looking for. He dodges pillars and pedestrians and bounces off other cars in his mad pursuit.

In the 1980 film, "Blues Brothers," there are what may be the most car chase scenes and crashes in any movie. Cars pile on top of each other, an upside-down police car slides through an intersection on its roof, and another flies through the air, landing on the back of a truck.

Then there's the car chase scene in 1968's "Bullitt" on San Francisco's narrow streets and steep hills.

And, let's not omit 2001's "The Fast and Furious" with a chase leading to a slimmed-down car going under a 16-wheel tractor-trailer.

The only modern movie
without spoken words (almost)

Since the late 1930s, all general-release feature films have had spoken dialogue—with one exception.

Leave it to Mel Brooks. In 1976 he made a film called "Silent Movie," which had no spoken words except for this ingenious twist:

Brooks had the famous mime Marcel Marceau, who never talks while performing, utter the only word in the picture.

The scene was set up when Marceau is asked (by subtitles) to appear in a silent movie. Marceau speaks, and says, "non." The person asking, replies (by subtitles) "I don't know what he said. I don't understand French."

"Silent Movie" had a cast including Brooks, Sid Caesar, Marty Feldman, Bernadette Peters, Burt Reynolds, Paul Newman, Liza Minnelli, and Brooks' wife, Anne Bancroft, all doing silent comedy.

The first time
the ultimate 4-letter expletive
was used in a movie

From the time talkies began in 1927, it took 40 years before any actor uttered the "F" word on screen in a mainstream film.

It was said in a British film called, "I'll Never Forget Whatshisname," released in 1967.

The word was used by an actress with the unlikely name of Marianne Faithfull.

Ms. Faithfull made movie history of sorts with the use of that particular profanity.

Also in that film, by the way, was the famous American actor, Orson Welles.

The movie, about an advertising executive struggling with integrity, was largely forgettable—except for that one word that opened the floodgates for the use of any obscenity on screen.

The all-time cult movie

In 1970, an out-of-work actor, Richard O'Brien, in desperate straits for money, wrote an outrageous musical comedy about cross-dressing aliens.

He called it "The Rocky Horror Show," and somehow got it produced on a London stage.

It was a surprising hit, and then was moved to Los Angeles where it was also successful.

20th Century-Fox decided to make a movie out of it in 1975, and called it "The Rocky Horror Picture Show." It starred a young Susan Sarandon along with Tim Curry, Barry Bostwick and the singer Meat Loaf.

The film bombed.

But its producer, Lou Adler, still had faith in it—and he got an idea. He talked a theater in New York's Greenwich Village into running it at midnight on weekends.

What happened was that audiences not only came to see it—but they turned it into an audience-participation show. They came back week after week and knew the dialogue so well,

26

they shouted the lines at the actors on the screen. When it rained in the movie, the audience put newspapers over their heads in the theater. In a wedding scene, they threw rice at the screen. When the song "Time Warp" was played, they danced in the aisles. People came to the movie dressed like the characters in the film.

"The Rocky Horror Picture Show" spread across America with midnight showings and the same kind of audience participation.

The phenomenon has lasted for years, and turned the film—and its audiences—into one of the most unusual events in movie history.

Most characters played by one actor in one film

In "Kind Hearts and Coronets" (1949), a man attempts to murder eight different people who stand in his way for an inheritance.

Alec Guinness plays all eight victims—the most roles any one actor ever played in one movie.

The grand movie

One of the best movies ever made is rarely seen today (but well worth seeing if you can find it).

It was the 1932 film, "Grand Hotel"—that had one of the first all-star casts.

That cast included seven leading actors: Greta Garbo, John Barrymore, Joan Crawford, Lionel Barrymore, Wallace Beery, Jean Hersholt and Lewis Stone.

"Grand Hotel" won the Best Picture Oscar and featured one of the famous love scenes of all time between the two "Great Profiles," Garbo and John Barrymore.

Garbo and Barrymore are sitting on a bench facing each other—with their profiles prominent, in a scene to remember.

It's also the first movie in which Garbo uttered her trademark line that added to her mystique, "I vant to be alone."

Ethnic slurs— with a laugh

Mel Brooks' "Blazing Saddles" (1974), which he wrote, directed and acted in, used about every ethnic slur there is, but apparently because of the comedy involved, he got away with it. There was relatively little public criticism or demand that the film be boycotted, and it was a big box office success.

However, in these politically correct times, it's doubtful that Brooks could do it now.

Ethnic slurs aside, it was one of the funniest movies ever made. There's no question about Brooks' comedy talent. He had learned his trade as a comedian in Catskill hotels, then was one of the writers (with Woody Allen, Carl Reiner and Neil Simon) on Sid Caesar's popular TV show. It's a little-known fact that Brooks was also one of the creators of the long-running "Get Smart" TV series.

His major film before "Blazing Saddles" was "The Producers" in 1967. That was not a hit movie at the time, but gradually gathered a cult following, and then, of course, was turned into one of the biggest Broadway hits of all time—34 years after the movie was released.

The worst movie
ever made

You can probably think of many "favorites" in this category.

If you eliminate B movies and others with no pretensions, and concentrate only on major, mainstream films, our "winner" for this award is "The Babe Ruth Story."

Made in 1948, and starring William Bendix and Claire Trevor, the movie was anticipated to be another "Pride of the Yankees."

That very good film about Babe's teammate, Lou Gehrig, and Gehrig's struggles with amyotrophic lateral sclerosis, the disease that came to be named for him, is considered one of the best sports movies ever made. It transcends sports with sensitive performances by Gary Cooper and Teresa Wright.

But "The Babe Ruth Story" is something else. Although Ruth was one of the greatest and most popular U.S. sports figure ever, the movie, which had so much to work with, was a dismal flop at the box office, and with the public and critics.

Bendix not only didn't capture the larger-than-life Ruth, but he didn't even throw like a ballplayer. (Why the director didn't use a double for those scenes is a mystery).

The deathbed scene is full of, as one critic said, sap and over-sentimentality, and should be avoided at all costs.

One interesting note:

The funny thing is that Bendix, who was a veteran actor, actually had known Ruth very well. As a kid, Bendix was the Yankees' batboy when Ruth was a player, and Bendix was involved in a famous incident with the Babe.

Ruth missed several games with a well-publicized stomach ache. His illness was caused by eating an estimated 10 hot dogs at one sitting. The boy who went out to buy the hot dogs for Ruth in real life was... William Bendix.

What was the greatest love scene?

There have been so many great love scenes in movie history, it's difficult to pick the best one, but we offer this as one solid candidate:

In "From Here to Eternity" (1953), Burt Lancaster is an Army sergeant stationed in Hawaii just before the Pearl Harbor attack.

He falls in love with an officer's wife, Deborah Kerr, and she with him.

Lancaster, a perfect soldier up till then, risks his career, and worse, by going out with Kerr. A friend of Lancaster tells him that he, an enlisted man, can wind up in prison for fooling around with the wife of an officer. Lancaster well knows the rules, but he goes ahead anyway.

He and the love-starved Kerr meet on a Hawaiian beach for a magnificent scene in the surf as ocean tides roll over them.

Their surfside embrace, lying on the sand as the tide rolls out, their bodies wet from the ocean water, has been called one of the most passionate ever.

The immortal
stateroom scene

In "A Night at the Opera" with the Marx Brothers (1935), Groucho is in a stateroom on a ship—except it isn't really a stateroom. Groucho is given a room that's just a little bigger than a closet.

What follows is one of the great comedy scenes.

First his large steamer trunk is brought to the room. He opens it and out come stowaways Chico and Harpo and their friend, Allan Jones. That's four people and the trunk in the room—but that's only the beginning.

Next come two maids to make the bed jammed into the space. Then an engineer and the engineer's assistant. Then a manicurist for Groucho. Then a guest. Then a cleaning man. Then three waiters with trays of food. That's 14 people.

Groucho manages to shut the door with everybody inside. But along comes Margaret Dumont to see Groucho. She walks down the hall, opens the door—and all 14 people fall out, ending the outrageous scene.

33

The antiwar classic

Hollywood has made many great war movies, but one of the first Oscar winners for Best Picture was a film many critics say was the best antiwar movie ever made.

It was the 1930 picture, "All Quiet on the Western Front," starring Lew Ayers.

The last scene in this film is a classic unto itself.

Ayers is in the trenches during World War I. Following graphic depictions of the horrors of war, there's a lull in the fighting. The sun is shining, and all is quiet on the battlefield, except for a few birds chirping. The world actually looks peaceful and beautiful again for a moment.

Just then a pretty butterfly flies by. Ayers, who plays a young schoolboy at the start of the war, rises up from his trench to catch the butterfly in his fingers so he can admire its loveliness.

A shot rings out. Ayers falls. Another young life is snuffed out.

Ayers was so affected by this movie that he became a conscientious objector in World War II, effectively ending his successful movie career. Studios wouldn't hire him and theaters wouldn't have shown his pictures anyway.

After "All Quiet on the Western Front" but before World War II, Ayers had been hugely popular in the series of nine "Dr. Kildare" movies in which he played the title role opposite Lionel Barrymore's Dr. Gilllespie.

"All Quiet on the Western Front" was the movie that made a star out of Ayers, and then, ironically, because he felt the film's message so deeply, it took his stardom away from him.

War movie wins
first Oscar

Two years before "All Quiet on the Western Front" won an Oscar, a war movie, with spectacular World War I air battles, was honored as the first film ever to win Best Picture at the Academy Awards.

It was "Wings," starring Clara Bow, Buddy Rogers and Richard Arlen, and, in a bit part, future star Gary Cooper.

He was older
than his mother

One of the top 100 movies of all time, according to the American Film Institute, was the 1942 film, "Yankee Doodle Dandy." Its star, who won the Oscar as Best Actor that year, was James Cagney—but there's an oddity connected with that.

Cagney was 43 years old at the time. The woman who played his mother, Rosemary DeCamp, was only 28.

Despite being 15 years younger than her "son," she gave a convincing performance as Cagney's mother.

If you didn't know their ages, you would never guess that she was really that much younger than Cagney.

Of course, makeup helped.

Top movies that
never won the Oscar

It's surprising how many films that are considered classics and/or all-time favorites never won the Best Picture Oscar at the Academy Awards.

Among the movies that failed to get the Best Picture prize are:

"Citizen Kane"
"Singin' in the Rain"
"Sunset Boulevard"
"The Graduate"
"The Wizard of Oz"
"It's a Wonderful Life"
"Star Wars"
"Chinatown"
"The Grapes of Wrath"
"2001: A Space Odyssey"
"E.T. The Extra Terrestrial"
"High Noon"
"Doctor Zhivago"
"Jaws"
"Fargo"
"L.A. Confidential"
"Saving Private Ryan"

TWO

Close-ups

Was Clark Gable his real name? —
and other stories of the stars

Was Clark Gable his real name?

Many movie stars change their names for better-sounding ones—but one of the biggest stars, whose name sounded like it could have been made-up, used his real name...sort of.

Clark Gable was born ~~William~~ Clark Gable in Cadiz, Ohio, in 1901. He dropped the ~~William~~ and became, arguably, the biggest male star in Hollywood history.

Gable appeared in over 50 movies from the 1930s to the 1960s—most of them big hits. He won an Oscar for "It Happened One Night," and made such other memorable movies as "Mutiny on the Bounty," "San Francisco," "Saratoga," and "Gone With the Wind," playing opposite the cream of Hollywood's female crop—Joan Crawford, Greta Garbo, Claudette Colbert, Greer Garson, Norma Shearer, Jean Harlow, Vivien Leigh, and finally, Marilyn Monroe.

The one movie he made with Monroe turned out to be his—and Monroe's—last. The film, "The Misfits," was shot in 1960. Gable died of a heart attack before it was released. He was only 59. Monroe died soon after, apparently from an overdose of sleeping pills. She was only 36.

Which actor was in the most movies?

In his long career in Hollywood, John Wayne set the record for playing in more films than any other star.

Wayne was in more than 200 movies from 1927 to 1976.

How popular was Wayne? In a 25-year period from the 1940s into the 1960s, he landed in the Top Ten in box office polls every year but one.

Born in Winterset, Iowa, in 1907, John Wayne's real name was Marion Morrison. He earned a football scholarship at the University of Southern California where he played two years before a shoulder injury ended his sports career.

During summers at Southern Cal he got a job at the Fox studios in the prop department. He met director John Ford who promised to put him in the movies. His first film was "The Drop Kick" in 1927.

The next year, director Raoul Walsh needed an actor for a western movie, "The Big Trail." Gary Cooper, who was supposed to play the part, became unavailable and Ford recommended Marion Morrison. Walsh gave him a screen test, hired him—and changed Morrison's name to John Wayne.

Walsh took the last name of Civil War general "Mad Anthony" Wayne, and added John because, he said, it sounded like a good American name.

The famous nickname Duke came from the name of Wayne's dog.

Wayne went on to specialize in western movies, but he got his first Oscar nomination for the patriotic "Sands of Iwo Jima" in 1949. He finally won his only Oscar as Best Actor in "True Grit" in 1969, but he had been a winner at the box office for many years before that.

Wayne's last film, "The Shootist" in 1976, was a poignant goodbye. Wayne dies at the end of the movie—knowing he himself is dying of cancer.

Just before his death, he became one of the few actors ever to have a congressional medal awarded in his honor.

The New York Times described Wayne as "the greatest figure of one of America's greatest native art forms, the western."

Down to his last $100,
he becomes a star overnight

Show business legends are full of stories about people becoming stars overnight. Some are fiction—but in the case of Sylvester Stallone, it really happened in a storybook way.

Ever since his high school days in Philadelphia, Stallone wanted to be a famous actor and screenwriter.

After graduation, he tried both. He wrote screenplays, but couldn't sell them. He landed a few minor roles in Hollywood movies, but couldn't make ends meet. Desperate, he took a role in at least one porno film.

He then decided to not only write a movie, but to try to sell it as a package with himself as the lead.

At this point in his life, he had a pregnant wife and, reportedly, about $100 in the bank. In three days he wrote the first draft of "Rocky," and sold it to producers Irwin Winkler and Robert Chartoff. The deal gave Stallone everything he wanted: his own script, his first starring role—and a large share of the profits, if any.

In stuff dreams are made of, "Rocky" became a big hit and Stallone became a star—and a wealthy man.

He was nominated for Academy Awards for Best Actor and Best Screenplay and his movie won the Oscar for Best Picture for 1976.

The story of the movie mirrored Stallone's life. The film was about a down-and-out boxer who wins against heavy odds.

Stallone went on to become one of the highest-paid actors in Hollywood. He starred in more "Rocky" movies, two "Rambo" films, and assorted others.

Movie star fights heavyweight champ

Victor McLaglen is unique in movie history. He's the only man to win an Oscar for Best Actor AND fight the heavyweight boxing champion of the world in real life.

McLaglen won his Oscar for "The Informer" in 1935. But before becoming an actor, he was a professional boxer in his native Great Britain.

He lasted six rounds in a fight against the world heavyweight champ, Jack Johnson.

The Hepburn women—
and a scathing classic review

Although Katharine Hepburn and Audrey Hepburn were not related, they shared more than their last names.

Both were from wealthy families, both were classy superstar movie actresses, and both won or were nominated for multiple Oscars.

Katharine was born to a prominent New England family. Her father was a noted surgeon and her mother a socially active crusader for women's rights. Katharine became active in theater in college, at Bryn Mawr.

Audrey's father was a British banker and her mother a Dutch baroness. Audrey studied ballet as a child and took acting lessons while attending upper-class English schools.

Katharine won Best Actress Oscars for "Morning Glory" (1933), "Guess Who's Coming to Dinner" (1967), "The Lion in Winter" (1968) and "On Golden Pond " (1981).

Audrey won the Best Actress Oscar for "Roman Holiday" in 1953 in her first starring role and was nominated for the award four other years.

One of the intriguing aspects of Katharine's life was her 27-year romance with her frequent co-star, Spencer Tracy. It was an open secret in Hollywood, but gossip columnists didn't write much about it out of respect to these two popular stars. Finally it became more public knowledge when writer-director Garson Kanin wrote his best-seller, "Tracy and Hepburn: An Intimate Memoir." Hepburn's one marriage ended in divorce years before she met Tracy, but Tracy was married during the Hepburn-Tracy affair, and Tracy's wife Louise became openly agitated when Hepburn spent long hours at Tracy's bedside during his fatal illness.

Audrey was married for 14 years to actor Mel Ferrer, and after their divorce, she married twice more, to an Italian psychiatrist and a Dutch actor.

One scathing review that Katharine got early in her career has become a classic. The critic Dorothy Parker, seeing Katharine in a New York play, wrote, "Katharine Hepburn runs the gamut of emotions from A to B." Otherwise, both Katharine and Audrey Hepburn got excellent reviews during their careers.

How many movies was Elvis Presley in?

Although Elvis Presley was better known for his hit records and personal appearances, he made a surprising number of movies.

Presley was in 33 films.

His first was "Love Me Tender" in 1956. His thirty-third was "Change of Habit" in 1969 (in which he plays a doctor who falls in love with a nun).

In between he was in such movies as "Jailhouse Rock" ((1957), "Viva Las Vegas" (1964) and "Frankie and Johnny" (1966).

He also played in two non-musicals, "Flaming Star" in 1960 and "Wild in the Country" in 1961.

Presley got especially good reviews as an actor in "Flaming Star."

Who looks like
Cary Grant?

Any list of good-looking movies stars has to include the suave, debonair Cary Grant who was in Hollywood movies for 34 years from 1932 to 1966, looking great in whatever role he played.

Grant's real name was Archibald Leach. He was born to a poor family in England, but came to America as a teenager, did some stage work, was spotted by a movie producer, and became a film legend.

One night in Hollywood, after he retired, Grant was invited to a benefit performance. He got to the theater and realized he had left his ticket at home. He went up to the ticket-taker and explained that he was sorry he had forgotten his ticket, and said, "I'm Cary Grant."

The skeptical ticket-taker said, "You don't look like Cary Grant.

Grant replied, "Who does?"

Who was the only actor to star in 2 of Top 10 films?

Of the Top 10 movies of all time as selected by the American Film Institute, the only actor who starred in more than one of them was Marlon Brando.

Brando was in the No. 3 movie, "The Godfather" in 1972, and the eighth best of all time, "On the Waterfront" in 1954.

It was in "On the Waterfront" that he delivered his unforgettable line, "I coulda been a contendah."

Brando was born in Omaha, Neb., where his mother had been an actress who played opposite Henry Fonda at the Omaha Community Playhouse.

Brando won the Best Actor Oscar for both "The Godfather" and "On the Waterfront," and he appeared in many other well-known films like "A Streetcar Named Desire," "Viva Zapata," "The Wild One," "Guys and Dolls," "The Teahouse of the August Moon," "Sayonara," "The Young Lions," "Mutiny on the Bounty," "The Ugly American," "Last Tango in Paris" and "Apocalypse Now."

The first great lover

Rudolph Valentino went from being a gardener and window washer to the most sensational romantic actor of the silent movies.

Such was his hold on audiences that when he died from a perforated ulcer at age 31 in 1926, thousands of fans lined the streets during his funeral in what has been called one of the biggest funeral outpourings of all time. Some fans fainted; police had trouble controlling the crowds; and supposedly, a few women in the country committed suicide over Valentino's sudden, unexpected death.

His short, legendary 8-year career included such movies as "The Sheik" and "Blood and Sand."

Looking at his films today, you may wonder what all the commotion was about. He tended to overact, with exaggerated eye movements and a flaring of nostrils.

But he had a brooding intensity and, apparently, a sensuous appeal that made him one of the first superstars in Hollywood.

51

Jack Nicholson
in obscurity

It's surprising now to know that superstar Jack Nicholson spent his first 11 years in Hollywood appearing only in minor "B" movies—and hardly anyone seemed to notice him or his talents.

He got his big break by chance when Rip Torn, who was supposed to be in "Easy Rider," couldn't make the picture. Producers, desperate for a replacement, gave the job to Nicholson as a last resort.

That 1969 film turned out to be a surprise hit and made a star of Nicholson. He milked the most out of his role of a dropout lawyer, and he won a nomination for Best Supporting Actor.

One year later he solidified his stardom in "Five Easy Pieces," with one of the great scenes of all time: In a diner, he tried to order a simple sandwich that was not on the menu. His repartee with the obstinate waitress was pure Nicholson and made movie highlight history. Nicholson won his first Best Actor Oscar nomination for that one and established his superstar status that has lasted more than 30 years.

Since then, Nicholson has played in a variety of interesting roles in such films as "Carnal Knowledge," "Chinatown," "One Flew Over the Cuckoo's Nest," "Terms of Endearment," "The Shining," "Prizzi's Honor," "As Good as it Gets," "About Schmidt," and "Anger Management."

Nicholson was born in Neptune, N.J., in 1937. He was raised by his mother who ran a beauty parlor after his alcoholic father deserted the family.

Jack finished high school but never attended college. He got to Hollywood when he visited a sister in California and took a job as a gopher at MGM.

That began his 11 years of obscurity in the movie capital until that "Easy Rider" break.

A movie saved
a fabulous career

Frank Sinatra was to the generation of teenagers in the 1940s what Elvis Presley and the Beatles were to future generations. He was as big a star as any who ever came along—but by the early '50s, his career seemed over, finished, gone.

His vocal chords had hemorrhaged, his agent dropped him, and audiences had turned to other stars.

Sinatra was suffering professionally, personally and financially.

Meantime, Columbia Pictures was casting its upcoming movie, "From Here to Eternity." Through some friends, Sinatra heard Columbia was looking for someone to play the role of Maggio in the 1953 film.

Sinatra went to Columbia's boss, Harry Cohn, and pleaded (some reports say "begged") for the part. Cohn, always known for hiring cheap talent when he could, made Sinatra an insulting offer of $8,000 for the role.

Sinatra accepted.

It turned out that Sinatra gave the performance of his life. He won the Oscar for Best Supporting Actor—and his career was back.

He then went on to play roles in other serious movies like "The Man With the Golden Arm,"—and his vocal chords healed so he could sing again, which he did in "Guys and Dolls" and "High Society."

By this time, Sinatra was regaining his superstar status.

He continued to make movies while also appearing on TV and headlining personal appearance shows in Las Vegas and elsewhere.

Thanks to that $8,000 Oscar and the resulting work, Sinatra swaggered to the top, became known as "The Chairman of the Board" (of show business), and one of the biggest names in entertainment…again.

Schwarzenegger:
the unlikely star

Of all the men who've become Hollywood movie stars, one of the least likely to attain that status is Arnold Schwarzenegger.

He had no acting experience. He kept his long last name, and he does not quite look like a Cary Grant or a Robert Redford.

But as a bodybuilding champion, he does have impressive muscles and has been perfect for the type of movie roles he's played.

Born in Austria in 1947, Schwarzenegger won the world championship in bodybuilding, along with titles of Mr. Europe and Mr. Olympia. Then he came to the U.S. in the 1970s to further his career as a bodybuilder. He made a promotional documentary film called "Pumping Iron."

That led to an offer to appear in movies, and by 1984 he was a big hit in "The Terminator." Other films followed and most have been box office successes.

Schwarzenegger achieved more fame with his marriage. Although he was a conservative Republican, he married into the liberal Kennedy family, wedding TV personality Maria Shriver.

Who was
Matuschanskayasky?

No movie star ever had to shorten his name as much as Walter Matuschanskayasky.

He was born in New York City in 1920 with that name, became a stage actor and then made his first movie in 1955. He starred in such films as "The Fortune Cookie," "The Bad News Bears" and "The Odd Couple."

You know him as Walter Matthau.

But he did play a character named Matuschanskayasky in a 1974 film, "Earthquake."

Some other
name changes

Judy Garland was born Frances Gumm, Mel Brooks was Melvin Kaminski, Woody Allen was Allen Konigsberg, Sandra Dee was Alexandra Zuck, Diana Dors was Diana Fluck, Cyd Charisse was Tula Finklea.

Marilyn Monroe was Norma Jean Mortenson, Tony Curtis was Bernard Schwartz, Anne Bancroft was Anna Maria Italiano, Joan Crawford was Lucille Le Suer, Greta Garbo was Greta Gustafsson.

He tried to create a star

With lots of money and relentless publicity, can someone turn an average actress into a big star?

Media tycoon William Randolph Hearst made a bet that he could do just that.

Hearst was rich; he owned a string of big-city newspapers, national magazines, and a worldwide news service.

He took a romantic interest in a young, blonde movie starlet, Marion Davies and vowed to make her, as he said, "The greatest star in Hollywood."

He founded a film company, Cosmopolitan Pictures, for the sole purpose of producing her films.

Hearst sent out orders to his newspapers and magazines to give her extensive publicity, only good reviews, and never to pan anything she did. Hearst's orders were law in his vast media empire.

Also, no mention was ever to be made of their romantic relationship.

Hearst was so powerful that he almost single-handily forced the United States into the Spanish-American War as a circulation booster.

Alas, despite all of Hearst's efforts, Davies never became a top movie star. She appeared in more than 40 films from 1917 to 1937, and although some neutral critics agreed she was pretty and had some talent, the public, partially turned off by Hearst's machinations, never really took to her.

Hearst and Davies lived together for years in the splendor of Hearst's famous mansion, San Simeon. They never married because Mrs. Hearst wouldn't give her husband a divorce.

The Hearst-Davies story is part of the semi-biographical movie on Hearst—the movie some consider the greatest of all time, "Citizen Kane."

Among the orders Hearst gave his newspapers and magazines was to call Davies "a vision of loveliness," "a bewitching beauty," and to write that her pictures were "movie masterpieces."

Hearst had bet that he could make Davies a star—but he lost.

Eddie Murphy
had the right genes

One of Eddie Murphy's first big hits was when he played a cop in "Beverly Hills Cop" in 1984.

Murphy came by the part naturally. His father had been a policeman in New York City, though it's doubtful that Eddie's father was as funny on the job as Eddie was in the movie.

Eddie Murphy broke into show business doing comedy routines in local New York clubs while he was still in high school.

He hit the big time when he won an audition to appear on TV's "Saturday Night Live." He was an instant success on that show, and then it was off to Hollywood.

His first movie was "48 Hours" in 1982. Then in 1983, he starred in "Trading Places," and the next year went back to his roots in "Beverly Hills Cop."

Look what
he overcame

Sammy Davis Jr., whose movie credits included "Ocean's 11," "Porgy and Bess," "Sergeants Three" and "Robin and the Seven Hoods," overcame extraordinary obstacles to become a leading entertainer.

He was born in Harlem, rarely went to school, lost an eye in a near-fatal auto crash, had several hip surgeries, became addicted to alcohol and cocaine, was a compulsive gambler and spender (an estimated $50 million over 20 years), endured ugly slurs over his interracial marriage to actress Mae Britt, and suffered from throat cancer.

Despite all that, Davis almost always showed a happy face in his successful career as a singer, dancer and actor.

He was also well known as a member in good standing in the exclusive clique, "The Rat Pack" that included fellow entertainers Frank Sinatra, Dean Martin, Joey Bishop and Peter Lawford.

The First Ladies in the movies

Two women who would later occupy the White House as First Ladies were actresses in Hollywood.

Pat Nixon had bit parts in several films—including a historic one. She was in "Becky Sharp" in 1935. That was the first full-length movie shot in Technicolor.

Then there was Ronald Reagan's wife—and the United States could have had a Best Actress Oscar-winner as First Lady.

Reagan was married to Jane Wyman who won the Oscar for her performance in "Johnny Belinda" in 1948. But Reagan and Wyman divorced shortly after the picture was made.

Reagan then married another movie actress, Nancy Davis, who would be his First Lady when he was president.

Davis had appeared in a few films, including one with Reagan, "Hellcats of the Navy," in 1957.

The "It" Girl

The first female superstar sex symbol in Hollywood history was Clara Bow who appeared in many movies in the 1920s.

One of her films was titled "It," and that's where she got her famous " It Girl" nickname.

In many ways she personified the liberated women of the Roaring '20s. Women copied her flapper-style of dress, makeup and hairstyle.

But just as the Roaring '20s came to a screeching halt with the 1930s Great Depression, so did Bow's career.

"The It Girl" became involved in several scandals over drugs, blackmail and adultery. And that was "it" for Clara Bow.

Near the end of her life, in the 1950s, she was finally heard from again. She was quoted as saying that she gave her old crown of "It Girl" to Marilyn Monroe.

There were 5—not 3— Marx Brothers

You may remember only three Marx Brothers—Groucho, Chico and Harpo—who starred in most of their movies, but when they started, there were two more brothers.

Zeppo dropped out after the first five of their 13 films and became his brothers' agent.

Gummo was part of the act when they were in vaudeville, but he never appeared in any of their films.

What were their real first names?

Groucho was Julius. Chico was Leonard. Harpo was Adolph. Zeppo was Herbert. And Gummo was Milton.

The reason Harpo never spoke in the movies is that in an early vaudeville show, a critic said Harpo was good as a mime and when playing his harp, but the magic was lost when he spoke. Harpo never talked again in the act (but there was nothing wrong with his speaking voice).

Harpo, by the way, was one of the few prominent male harpists in the world. Most harpists in major symphony orchestras are female.

Film fans usually pick these as the best Marx Brothers movies: "The Coconuts" (1929), "Animal Crackers" (1930), "Horsefeathers" (1932), "Duck Soup" (1933), "A Night at the Opera" (1935), "A Day at the Races" (1937) and "Room Service" (1938). Their last film together was "Love Happy" in 1949 (with Marilyn Monroe).

After that, only Groucho remained active in show business, becoming a radio and TV star with "You Bet Your Life."

Groucho, who smoked cigars all his adult years, was once told by his doctor to give them up. Goucho's son came to dinner sometime after that and noticed his father was still smoking. "What about that doctor who told you to stop smoking?" the son asked. Groucho replied, "He died." Groucho lived to age 87, dying in 1977.

Another great Groucho line was uttered on his TV show. A woman contestant told Groucho she had 15 children. "Fifteen!" Groucho said. "Why so many?" The woman said, "I love my husband." Groucho replied, on TV, "I love my cigar, but I take it out once in a while."

He did a lot of eating

Robert De Niro, who studied method acting under the legendary Stella Adler and Lee Strasberg, is known for deeply immersing himself into any part he plays—and he had an unusual assignment to get ready for this role: He was to play the aging boxing champion Jake LaMotta in "Raging Bull" in 1980.

De Niro had to gain 60 pounds to accurately depict the boxer's decline from a champion to a bloated has-been. De Niro went from his normal weight of 150 pounds to 210.

According to the Guinness Book of World Records, that's the most weight any actor ever gained for a film appearance.

It paid off for De Niro. He won his first Best Actor Oscar.

At the other end of the scale (literally), Jennifer Jason Leigh lost an undisclosed amount of weight to get down to 86 pounds to play an anorexic teenager in 1986's "The Best Little Girl in the World."

Cagney's immortal scene

James Cagney was one of Hollywood's most versatile actors. He was a great song-and-dance man, as he showed in his Oscar award-winning performance in "Yankee Doodle Dandy," but he could also play tough, ruthless gangsters.

His first fame came in the 1931 movie, "Public Enemy." The scene in that film that made him famous was when he was having an argument with actress Mae Clarke—and Cagney shoved half a grapefruit into her face.

Not a nice thing to do, but it made Cagney a star, and he was cast in many succeeding gangster roles.

Cagney's versatility can be seen in the contrast of being able to play low-life hoodlums as well as a good-citizen, flag-waving patriot (with superstar singing and dancing, as he did in "Yankee Doodle Dandy.").

His real life mirrored his film roles. Cagney grew up in a crime-ridden New York City neighborhood where he had to learn to fight, and then he began his show business career as a singer and dancer in vaudeville and on the Broadway stage.

The unusual career
of Jodie Foster

Many child stars fade into oblivion when they grow up. Jodie Foster not only didn't do that— but she was playing amazing adult roles before reaching age 14.

In early childhood, Foster appeared in several movies, was on Walt Disney TV shows, made her first feature film at age 9 in "Napoleon and Samantha"—and AT AGE 12 was cast as a prostitute opposite Robert De Niro in "Taxi Driver." That popular film, and her unbelievable performance, vaulted her into national prominence.

Again playing roles beyond her years, she was a speakeasy queen in "Bugsy Malone" before she reached her 14th birthday.

Foster made a few more movies in her teenage years, including one in France in which she spoke fluent French. Then she enrolled at Yale University where "Taxi Driver" bizarrely came back to haunt her. A man named John Hinckley Jr. had been infatuated with Foster in

"Taxi Driver," and in 1981, trying to reenact a scene from the movie, Hinckley attempted to assassinate President Ronald Reagan—saying his primary motive was his desire to impress Foster.

Although Foster was obviously shaken by that incident, she went on to graduate magna cum laude from Yale.

Foster returned to Hollywood where she picked up her movie career as an adult, winning Best Actress Oscars for "The Accused" in 1988 and "The Silence of the Lambs" in 1991. She appeared in the thriller, "Panic Room" in 2002, and has also directed several films.

One other note about the amazing career of Jodie Foster. At age 3, as a model, she was the bare-bottomed "Coppertone Girl" (with a dog pulling down the back of her bathing suit).

The picture of that appeared on billboards and in newspaper ads across the country. It became one of the most famous advertising campaigns of all time.

The fighting sisters

Olivia and Joan De Havilland were born into a prominent, wealthy family that had been in America since Colonial days.

Joan changed her last name to Fontaine when both women became movie stars.

And then the trouble started.

Both were nominated for the Best Actress Oscar in 1941—Olivia De Havilland for "Hold Back the Dawn" and Joan Fontaine for "Suspicion."

Joan won the award. That touched off a well-publicized sisterly feud that lasted for years.

Olivia finally triumphed over her sister when Olivia won Best Actress for "To Each His Own" in 1946. Joan was on hand to congratulate her sister at the Oscar ceremony, but Olivia publicly and brusquely brushed her off.

That was out of character of perhaps Oliva's best-remembered screen role today—the sweet, understanding Melanie in "Gone With the Wind."

The surprising
acting performance

Harold Russell was a disabled veteran of World War II. He lost both hands in a wartime accident. He had never been an actor—and had never taken an acting lesson.

But he was given the role, on a fluke, of playing a returning sailor in the highly-acclaimed movie, "The Best Years of Our Lives" in 1946.

The film's director, William Wyler, had seen Russell demonstrate using his prosthetic steel hooks that replaced his hands and urged producer Sam Goldwyn to cast Russell in the movie. Goldwyn was opposed to the idea, based on Russell's lack of experience, but Wyler insisted, and won out.

What happened? Russell won the Academy Award for Best Supporting actor. Wyler later said that Russell "gave the finest performance I have ever seen on the screen."

Russell earned less than $10,000 for his performance and had no rights to the film's residual profits. However, after the movie's success, Goldwyn, somewhat generously, offered Russell $120 a week for a year to make promotional appearances.

He was Moses, Michelangelo, Buffalo Bill & Ben-Hur

No actor in Hollywood history played more famous people than Charlton Heston.

In addition to being Moses in "The Ten Commandments," Michelangelo in "The Agony and the Ecstasy," Buffalo Bill in "Pony Express," and Ben-Hur in "Ben-Hur," he played El Cid in "El Cid," President Andrew Jackson in "The Buccaneer," Clark of the Lewis and Clark expedition in "Far Horizons," John the Baptist in "The Greatest Story Ever Told," Anthony in "Anthony and Cleopatra" and Cardinal Richelieu in "The Three Musketeers."

In all he made over 50 films in his amazing half-century career that started in the 1950s, and it seems when any historical movie spectacular came along, directors thought of Heston first.

He won the Best Actor Oscar for "Ben-Hur" in 1959.

Heston's real last name was Carter but he changed it to his stepfather's name, Heston, after studying acting at Northwestern University. He began playing in regional theaters and on Broadway before coming to Hollywood where his first big role was in "The Greatest Show on Earth." That title seemed to presage his ultimate career playing larger-than-life figures.

Off the screen, he was also visible as president of the Screen Actor's Guild (a job once held by Ronald Reagan), chairman of the American Film Institute, and president of the National Rifle Association. Like Reagan, Heston became a victim of Alzheimer's disease.

They finished the picture without her

One of the brightest stars of Hollywood in the 1930s was Jean Harlow, known as the "Platinum Blonde Bombshell."

But while filming "Saratoga" with Clark Gable in 1937, she became ill with uremic poisoning, and died—at the age of 26.

The movie was juggled to finish it with a double. In scenes which Harlow was unable to complete, the director showed only her double's back, and a stand-in's voice was used.

Call him
Mister

In a bit of pretentious public relations, film companies started billing the actor Paul Muni as "Mr. Paul Muni."

Muni was unquestionably a good actor both on stage and screen and played a variety of roles in the movies, especially in the 1930s.

He won the Best Actor Oscar for "The Story of Louis Pasteur" in 1936.

But perhaps his most powerful performance was in "I Am a Fugitive From a Chain Gang" in 1933. He also was impressive in "The Life of Emile Zola," "Juarez," and "The Good Earth."

However it still looked odd to see his name listed as "Mr. Paul Muni" on movie marquees and in newspaper ads.

No other star ever got such billing.

Steve Martin was a magician first

Steve Martin entered show business—not as a comedian—but as a magician. He performed in a magic act around Southern California.

As time went on, Martin began adding jokes to his magic routines, and a new career was born.

He got an assignment to write comedy sketches for the Smothers Brothers TV show.

That led him to "Saturday Night Live" as a writer and performer, and he was on his way.

Martin entered the movies by writing and starring in "The Jerk" in 1979. It was a big hit, and established him in films with his unique kind of comedy.

Other movies followed, including "Dead Men Don't Wear Plaid" (1982), "The Man With Two Brains" (1983), "Little Shop of Horrors" (1986), "Planes, Trains and Automobiles" (1987), "Parenthood" (1989), "Father of the Bride" (1991), "Mixed Nuts" (1994) "Father of the Bride, Part II" (1995), "Joe Gould's Secret" (1999) and "The Out-of-Towners" (1999).

Martin had found his comedy magic on the screen.

The fascinating career of Shirley Temple

By the age of 6, Shirley Temple displayed incredible acting, singing and dancing ability that could put grown-up stars to shame. As a child, Shirley really could act, sing and dance at a high professional level.

And even at that age, she not only memorized all her lines perfectly, but also knew everyone else's, too.

If Mozart was a child-genius in serious music, Shirley Temple must be considered a child-genius in popular movie making.

Between the ages of 6 and 10, from 1934 to 1938, she was making three to four feature movies a year, rescuing the Fox studios from financial disaster in those Depression years.

Few stars—young or old—ever reached the fame or popularity that Shirley achieved.

There were Shirley Temple dolls, coloring books, dresses, and drinks. ("Shirley Temples" are still a non-alcoholic bar drink for children today).

But—by 1940, at the age of 12, she was a movie has-been.

Her immense natural talent as a child star did not carry over with audiences when she approached her teens.

She tried some movie roles in the 1940s and then some unsuccessful TV work in the 1950s and '60s—but the spark was gone.

Turning away from show business, Shirley entered politics.

She ran unsuccessfully for a Congressional seat, then was appointed the U.S. representative to the U.N. by President Nixon and later U.S. ambassador to Ghana.

Meantime, she had married a wealthy business executive, Charles Black—and she became known in her high society social circles, not as Shirley Temple anymore, but as Mrs. Black.

One last note: A reporter once asked Shirley when she stopped believing in Santa Claus. She said it was when her mother took her to see Santa in a department store when she was 7, and he asked her for her autograph.

The movie career
of a president

The 40th president of the United States, Ronald Reagan, appeared in more than 50 movies during his 27-year career as an actor in Hollywood.

He started his adult life as a radio announcer on station WHO in Des Moines, Iowa, then came to Hollywood and won a role as a radio announcer in his first film, "Love Is on the Air" in 1937.

Reagan was in two more "B" pictures, and then moved up to an "A" film, "Brother Rat," about cadets at a military school. That movie and Reagan's performance were popularly received.

Next came what was probably his most famous role. He played the college football Hall of Famer George Gipp in "Knute Rockne, All American," in 1940. That was the movie in which Reagan created one of the great scenes in film history.

Lying on his deathbed after becoming ill at the end of the season, Gipp (Reagan) told Coach Knute Rockne of Notre Dame:

"I've got to go now, Rock. It's all right. But sometime, Rock, when the team's up against it; when things are wrong and the breaks are beating the boys, tell them to go in there with all they've got—and win one for the Gipper. I don't know where I'll be then, but I'll know it, Rock, and I'll be smiling."

In real life, that speech was used by Coach Rockne at halftime of the Notre Dame-Army game in 1928, and it became the most famous pep talk in football history. (Notre Dame rallied to win).

But also in real life, when he was U.S. president, Reagan turned "winning one for the Gipper" into one of his favorite sayings.

The remainder of his film career was rather pedestrian, including a movie called "Bedtime for Bonzo" in 1951 that, besides Reagan as a college professor, featured a chimpanzee.

Reagan's last movie was "The Killers" in 1964.

Of all the different parts Reagan played in his more than 50 films, he never played a president. But 16 years after his last movie, he was elected to the highest office in the land and presided over major economic and military changes in the United States and the world.

The fastest fadeout in history of a successful movie career

The most incredible thing happened to Luise Rainer.

In the second movie she ever made in Hollywood, "The Great Ziegfeld" in 1936, she won the Oscar for Best Actress—and the next year, in the third movie she ever made, she won the Best Actress Oscar again for "The Good Earth." BUT, that was essentially the beginning and end of her meteoric career.

She was only 27 years old at the time, and you'd think that winning two Best Actress Oscars in a row would set her up for great, long success. She was, by the way, the first actor or actress to win Oscars in consecutive years.

Some movie historians blame her husband, playwright Clifford Odets, for picking bad films for her after "The Good Earth." Others blame MGM for rushing her into pictures with poor scripts, but whatever the cause, Rainer appeared in only six more movies—none of which were good for her or the box office.

She was finished as a movie star at age 33. She divorced Odets, and left Hollywood.

It has been called the fastest, most complete fadeout of a leading lady in cinema history.

Rainer's great scene

When Luise Rainer won her first Best Actress Oscar for "The Great Ziegfeld," there was a memorable scene that has been called one of the most perfect bits of acting ever to be caught on camera.

Rainer, playing Ziegfeld's divorced wife, Held, is talking on the phone to Ziegfeld, whom she still deeply loved.

Rainer, trying to put up a good front to hide her jealousy and sadness, congratulates Ziegfield on his coming marriage to Billie Burke.

One critic said that Rainer gave a performance "of unbearable poignancy—a veritable lesson in what a great artist can make of a single scene."

The actor who changed
the names of telephones

Dominic Amici was born in Kenosha, Wisc., became an actor at the University of Wisconsin, changed his name to Don Ameche, and went to Hollywood where he quickly became one of the busiest stars in the movies.

Ameche appeared in 34 films from the mid-1930s until the mid-'40s.

In 1939 he played the inventor of the telephone in "The Alexander Graham Bell Story." Ameche's performance captured the public's imagination. It became cool for people, especially teenagers, to start calling telephones "ameches," or to say, "I'll call you on the "ameche."

That fad, and Ameche's popularity, lasted for a while, but he was in so many films that he began to suffer from over-exposure. By the end of the '40s, his career seemed finished.

However, in later years, Ameche made some impressive comebacks. In 1985, at age 77, he won the Best Supporting Oscar for "Cocoon." Two years before that he had a great role opposite Eddie Murphy in "Trading Places."

But senior citizens will always remember him as Alexander Graham Bell.

What movie star had the longest career?

The all-time record holder is an actress whose movie career lasted from the time she was 16 years old until she was 91.

Who was she?

Answer is Lillian Gish who acted in her first movie in 1912 ("An Unseen Enemy"), and her last in 1987 ("The Whales of August").

In between, she was in movies in every decade. Besides her famous roles in "The Birth of a Nation" (1915) and "Orphans of the Storm" (1922), she appeared in later films like "His Double Life" (1933), "Duel in the Sun" (1946), "The Night of the Hunter" (1955), "The Comedians" (1967) and "A Wedding" (1978).

Her sister Dorothy also had a long run. Dorothy Gish was a movie actress from 1912 until her death in 1968.

But no one ever matched the incredible length of the 75-year Hollywood acting career of Lillian Gish.

What made Chaplin great? Looking past his comedy

There's no question that Charle Chaplin was one of the great comedians in screen history with his Little Tramp persona—but if you look beyond the comedy in his pictures, you see an actor capable of portraying tenderness, pathos, understanding, and even savage attacks on things he didn't like.

In "City Lights" (1931), his scenes with a blind girl are some of the most touching ever filmed.

Beneath the comedy in his "Modern Times" (1936), is his depiction of the dehumanizing effects of modern machinery.

His savage, comic attack on fascism in "The Great Dictator" (1940) makes this movie an all-time classic.

Chaplin had the rare gift of being both funny and profound at the same time. "He was the greatest artist ever to appear on the screen," said one Hollywood insider.

Incredibly, Chaplin never won the Oscar for his acting, or for his writing and directing. Finally, in 1972 he was given an honorary Academy Award. He came to the ceremony as a frail man of 82 and stood on stage to one of the largest and longest ovations in Academy Awards history.

The tears in his eyes, and the smile on his face, symbolized the roles he played so well in his movies.

He made magic with a balloon

An all-time great scene was created by Charlie Chaplin in "The Great Dictator" with a balloon.

Chaplin was playing a caricature of Adolph Hitler (and, oddly, there was an amazing real-life resemblance between Hitler and Chaplin, when Charlie wore his mustache).

In his office was a big balloon with a map of the world outlined on it.

Chaplin took the balloon, did an imaginative dance with it, kissed it, tapped it in the air with his hands and feet, and looked longingly at it as he dreams of world conquest.

It was pure Chaplin magic.

Chaplin didn't look
like Chaplin

In Monte Carlo in the 1940s, they staged a Charlie Chaplin look-alike contest. As a lark, the real Charlie Chaplin, who was staying in the area at the time, decided to enter the contest.

He came in third.

How Chaplin ate
those boots

One of the immortal Charlie Chaplin films was his "The Gold Rush," released in 1925.

Chaplin is in Alaska for the Klondike gold rush, living in harsh conditions.

He finds himself with no food to eat, so as a last resort, he takes off his boots and begins to bite into them, chew them and swallow them, stopping now and then to sprinkle on salt and pepper.

In a prolonged comedy scene, he seems to be enjoying chomping on his boots.

The way Chaplin was able to do this scene is that in reality, he had the boots made out of licorice.

Trick
question

What movie star died at the age of 14—
but left a son who also made movies?

Here's the answer:

He was the most popular movie star of
1926, according to a poll of theater owners that year.

He was…a dog named Rin Tin Tin—and
he was so popular he was often billed above human
actors in his films.

Rin Tin Tin appeared in some 15 movies
before his death at age 14, in 1932.

And then his son, Rin Tin Tin Jr., succeeded
him in several films through the 1930s.

A German shepherd, Rin Tin Tin starred in
such movies as "Jaws of Steel," "The Night Cry"
and "A Dog of the Regiment."

THREE

Gotcha...

Mistakes moviemakers made

Mistakes moviemakers made

- In the famous Battle of Atlanta scene in "Gone With the Wind," Vivien Leigh runs by an electric street light. Unfortunately, electric lights didn't exist during the Civil War.

- On Judy Garland's trip down the yellow brick road in "Wizard of Oz," the length of her hair changes three times.

- In the spectacular chariot race scene in "Ben-Hur," which takes place around the time of Christ, an automobile can be seen in the distance.

- When Bruce Willis makes a phone call in "Die Hard 2," he's at Dulles Airport, near Washington, D.C. But the pay phone he uses has Pacific Bell written on it.

- In the baseball movie, "Field of Dreams," Ray Liotta—who plays Shoeless Joe Jackson—bats right-handed. The real Shoeless Joe batted lefty.

Gotcha!

More mistakes
moviemakers made

- In the 1994 film, "Forrest Gump," there's a scene that's supposed to be taking place around 1970—but a person in the scene is reading a USA Today newspaper. USA Today didn't start publishing until 1982.

- Julia Roberts plays a character named Vivian in "Pretty Woman." She goes to an opera where an usher shows her to a seat—but instead of calling her Vivian, he calls her Julia.

- John Travolta is told in "Face/Off" that a bomb will go off in six days. The bomb shows the time left before it goes off. It reads 216 hours. That's nine days.

- In "The Two Jakes," set in 1948, Jack Nicholson is walking down the street and passes an automatic teller machine. There were no ATMs in 1948.

More mistakes

One cause of mistakes in movies is that individual scenes are shot at different times and often on different days. Also, scenes are not necessarily shot in the same sequence in which they will appear in the final version of the film.

Actors, directors and editors sometimes forget details—like in "The King and I," Yul Brynner is seen in a long shot wearing an earring. But in close-ups of the same scene, obviously shot at a different time, he has no earring.

In "Jaws," there's a scene that supposedly takes place on July 4. But there are no leaves on the trees because the scene was shot earlier in the year.

In "Viva Villa," Wallace Beery is awarded a medal at the end of the movie. The only problem is that he is seen wearing the same medal earlier in the movie, before he was given it.

Julia Roberts takes off Richard Gere's tie in a love scene in "Pretty Woman." Then in close-ups during that scene, the tie is back on.

FOUR

They Never Said It

And, the off-screen lines, too

They never said it

There are many famous, long-remembered, often-repeated lines from movies—but the problem is that some of them were never said on the screen.

- James Cagney never said, "You dirty rat!" in any film. Cary Grant never said, "Judy, Judy, Judy." Johnny Weissmuller never said, "Me Tarzan, you Jane."

- Perhaps the most misquoted movie line is "Play it again, Sam," from "Casablanca." Ingrid Bergman delivered the line, but she didn't say it that way. What she did say was, "Play it, Sam. Play 'As Time Goes By.'"

- For years Charles Boyer was famously quoted for saying, "Come with me to the Casbah," to Hedy Lamarr in "Algiers." You won't hear that line anywhere in the movie.

All this brings to mind Yogi Berra's quote, "I really didn't say everything I said."

Memorable
off-screen lines

Harry Cohn, head of Columbia Pictures for many years, was not a popular man. He was a tyrant with his actors, directors, writers and other employees. When he died in 1958, there was a huge turnout of movie people at his funeral. Red Skelton, looking at the casket holding Cohn, spoke for many when he said, "This large crowd proves that if you give the people something they want to see, they'll come to see it."

Oscar Levant, noticing that Doris Day was playing goody-goody girls in a string of movies, said, "I knew Doris BEFORE she was a virgin."

Then, there's the line when Katharine Hepburn first met Spencer Tracy as they were cast in the same film. Hepburn said, "Mr. Tracy, I think I'm too tall to play opposite you." Tracy replied, "Don't worry. I'll cut you down to size."

When Louis B. Mayer, head of MGM, saw the beautiful Ava Gardner's screen test, he said, "She can't act. She can't talk. She's terrific."

FIVE

Oscar Oddities

Why it's called the Oscar and
other Academy Awards stories

Why is it called
the Oscar?

When the Academy Awards started in 1929, the statuette given to winners was simply called the Academy Awards statuette.

Two years later, the academy's librarian, and later its executive director, Margaret Herrick, coined the name that became world famous.

She looked at the statuette one day and said, "You know, that looks like my Uncle Oscar"— actually a man named Oscar Pierce of Texas.

Herrick started referring to the statuette as Oscar, and the name caught on. Hollywood reporters were glad to have a name for it and they spread the word.

The irony is that Oscar Pierce himself had no connection with the movies. He was a real estate man—yet the best-known movie award is named for him.

First Oscar to win an Oscar

The first person named Oscar to win an Oscar was Oscar Hammerstein II.

Oscar won the Oscar for writing the lyrics to "The Last Time I Saw Paris" in the 1941 movie, "Lady Be Good."

Only actor to win 2 Oscars for SAME role

Harold Russell, the disabled World War II veteran who won the Oscar for Best Supporting Actor for the 1946 "Best Years of Our Lives," made Academy Awards history.

Besides his Best Supporting award, he received a second Oscar (an honorary one) "for bringing hope and courage to his fellow veterans."

That's the only time an actor got two Oscars for the same performance.

Upsets at Academy Awards

- Almost everybody assumed Clark Gable would win the Best Actor Oscar for his memorable performance in "Gone With the Wind" in 1939. But an actor who is little-remembered today, Robert Donat, took the award for his role in "Goodbye, Mr. Chips" that year. Many movie experts say that was the biggest Oscar upset ever.

- Then there were Humphrey Bogart and Ingrid Bergman in "Casablanca." They were sensational together——but although the film won Best Picture, neither Bogart nor Bergman won anything. Paul Lukas won Best Actor that year for "Watch on the Rhine," and Jennifer Jones won Best Actress for "The Song of Bernadette."

- And how about the film voted No. 1 as the best movie of all time by the American Film Institute——"Citizen Kane." It did NOT win Best Picture the year it was eligible, 1941. It was beaten by "How Green Was My Valley."

A tie for an Oscar?

What happens if two Academy Award nominees tie in the voting for an Oscar?

Do they flip a coin or pull a name out of the hat?

No. The academy gives each an Oscar—and it's happened three times.

In 1932 Frederick March (for "Dr. Jekyll and Mr. Hyde") and Wallace Beery (for "The Champ") tied for Best Actor.

In 1968, Katherine Hepburn (for "The Lion in Winter") and Barbra Streisand (for "Funny Girl") tied for Best Actress.

In 1927, Frank Borzage ("Seventh Heaven") and Lewis Milestone ("Two Arabian Knights") tied for Best Director.

Oddly, they never won

Surprisingly, many of Hollywood's most famous movie stars never won an Oscar for acting.

That list includes Greta Garbo, Cary Grant, Orson Welles, Charlie Chaplin, Richard Burton, Barbara Stanwyck and Judy Garland.

She married her "son," then had trouble keeping quiet

Greer Garson won the Best Actress Oscar for her sentimental role in "Mrs. Miniver" in 1942—and, oddly enough, during the filming of the movie, she fell in love with the man who played her son in the film, Richard Ney.

She married her "son" after the movie was released. While he was indeed younger than she, there wasn't that much difference in their ages. Garson was only 33 when she played the middle-aged mother in the movie, and he was in his 20s. The film's producers tried to keep news of the marriage quiet, but word leaked out.

Then a bizarre event happened at the Academy Awards ceremony. Garson accepted her Oscar and proceeded to give the longest acceptance speech in academy history. Nobody seemed able to stop her. She rambled on and on and on. There was no official timing of her speech, but some say it lasted more than half an hour.

After Garson's award, the academy passed new rules intended to limit the time of acceptance speeches.

Youngest to win acting Oscar

Who was the youngest person ever to win an Academy Award for acting?

The answer is Tatum O'Neal. She won the Oscar for Best Supporting Actress in 1973 for her role in "Paper Moon." She was just 9 years old when she made that movie.

Shirley Temple had won an Oscar when she was 6—but that was not for Best Actress or Best Supporting Actress. It was an honorary miniature Oscar for her big box office films that helped Hollywood in the Great Depression years.

O'Neal's Oscar was the real McCoy, as she was competing for the award against adult actresses.

Sad saga of James Dean

James Dean starred in only three movies in his life—"East of Eden," "Rebel Without a Cause" and "Giant"—and was nominated for Oscars for two of them ("Eden" and "Giant").

But then his promising career ended. He was killed in a car crash in 1955, at age 24.

He came so close
so many times

Al Pacino was a virtually unknown actor in the early 1970s when director Francis Ford Coppolo took a big gamble on him to play Michael Corleone in "The Godfather."

It was the first major film for Pacino, and he, and the movie, were mega-hits.

Pacino was nominated for the Best Supporting Actor Oscar, but didn't win it—and that started a unique streak for Pacino.

He was nominated for an Oscar four straight years, and went home empty-handed each time.

Aside from his "Godfather" nomination in 1972, he was also nominated for Best Actor for "Serpico" in 1973, "Godfather Part II" in 1974, and "Dog Day Afternoon" in 1975—but lost out for an Oscar for all of them.

Finally, Pacino's non-winning streak ended. He took home the Best Actor Oscar for "Scent of a Woman" in 1992.

The sweetest revenge

Julie Andrews was unquestionably a popular, great performer in the Broadway hit musical, "My Fair Lady," playing opposite Rex Harrison.

But when it came time to make a movie of "My Fair Lady" in 1964, Andrews, who had a wonderful singing voice, was passed over. The part was given to Audrey Hepburn...who couldn't sing. (Marni Nixon's voice was dubbed in for Hepburn's songs in the movie).

There was a large hue and cry over denying Andrews the role she successfully created on Broadway. But the movie producers wanted Hepburn.

Came Oscar time—and, although Rex Harrison won Best Actor for "My Fair Lady," Audrey Hepburn did not win Best Actress. The winner was, of all people, Julie Andrews, who had made "Mary Poppins" (instead of "My Fair Lady") that year.

Some film people and fans thought academy voters gave the Oscar to Andrews out of sympathy for the fact that she was passed over for "My Fair Lady." But Andrews was plenty good in "Mary Poppins."

In any case, Andrews had her revenge against the "My Fair Lady" producers—and then she showed them up again the next year with a classic performance in the movie, "The Sound of Music."

Strange moment at the Oscars

At the Academy Awards ceremonies in 1942, it came time to announce the winner for Best Song.

The famous songwriter, Irving Berlin, was asked to make the presentation.

Irving Berlin opened the envelope and said, the winner is...

"Irving Berlin, for his song 'White Christmas' in "Holiday Inn.""

As far as we know in our research, that's the only time a winner announced himself.

No suspense at
first Academy Awards

When the first Academy Awards ceremonies were held on May 16, 1929, everybody knew in advance who would win.

The winners' names had already been published in February, right after the votes were tallied.

They didn't get the idea to keep the winners a secret, and thereby build interest in the ceremonies, until the second year.

That second Academy Awards ceremony was the first to be broadcast, although it was carried only on one local Los Angeles radio station.

First time the ceremonies were on television was in 1953.

The first winning picture in Academy history was the story of World War I air battles, titled "Wings." That was also the only silent movie ever to win Best Picture.

The first to win Oscars for Best Actor and Best Actress were Emil Jannings and Janet Gaynor.

African-Americans
break the ice

The first black ever to win an Oscar was Hattie McDaniel for her role as Mammy in "Gone With the Wind" in 1939. McDaniel won Best Supporting Actress.

The first black performer to win for a leading role was Sidney Poitier who won Best Actor for "Lilies of the Field," in 1963.

Halle Berry
breaks barrier

From the beginnings of the Academy Awards in the 1920s, until 2001, no African-American woman had won the Best Actress Oscar.

That barrier was finally broken when Halle Berry won for her role in "Monster's Ball."

The first black to win Best Supporting Actor was Lou Gossett Jr., for "An Officer and a Gentleman" in 1982.

111

Anything can happen on live TV

Perhaps the most bizarre thing that ever happened during the telecast of the Academy Awards was in 1973.

A man using a fake press pass got backstage, took off all his clothes, and streaked naked across the stage and in front of TV cameras.

David Niven, on camera as a presenter at the time, came up with a quick ad lib. Niven said, "Isn't it fascinating that probably the only laugh this man will ever get in his life is by stripping off his clothes and showing his shortcomings."

Niven's remark got tremendous laughter and applause, and the show continued. The streaker was apprehended.

Tom Hanks ties record

When Tom Hanks won the Best Actor Oscar for "Forrest Gump" in 1994, after winning it the previous year for "Philadelphia," he became the first to win Best Actor two straight years since Spencer Tracy in 1937 and 1938.

Tracy had won in consecutive years for "Captains Courageous" and "Boys Town."

They refused
the Oscar

George C. Scott was nominated as Best Actor for his role in "Patton" in 1971—but before the Academy Awards were handed out, Scott said if he won, he would not accept the Oscar.

He said he was against the system of choosing winners and losers. Despite his stand, he won the award anyway, and the producer of "Patton," Frank McCarthy, accepted it for him. McCarthy said it proved the Academy was unbiased in its choices.

The next person to refuse the Oscar was Marlon Brando who won for "The Godfather" in 1972. Brando said he was against Hollywood's depiction of American Indians and he sent a native-American, Sacheen Littlefeather, to accept his award. She read a speech from Brando that castigated Hollywood for, as he said, "degrading Indians."

The Academy made one subtle change in recent years to diffuse the idea of winners and losers. The Academy asked presenters, when they open the envelopes, not to say, "And the winner is…", but to say, "And the Oscar goes to…".

It's heavier than
it looks

Academy Award winners are often surprised when they're handed an Oscar and discover it's heavier than they thought.

The Oscar weighs eight-and-a-half pounds. It stands just over 13 inches tall and is made of solid metal, electroplated with 18-karat gold.

Actress wins Oscars
48 years apart

Amazingly, Katharine Hepburn won a Best Actress Oscar in 1981—48 years after she won her first one.

Hepburn won in '81 for her performance in "On Golden Pond." She won her first Oscar in 1933 for "Morning Glory."

She also won two in between—for "Guess Who's Coming to Dinner" in 1967 and for "The Lion in Winter" in 1968.

Whooping
it up

The first woman to host the Academy Awards telecast was the African-American actress with the unlikely name, Whoopi Goldberg.

She hosted the Oscars for the first time in 1994—and that isn't her real name.

Goldberg was born Caryn Elaine Johnson in New York City. She changed her name, she said, because she thought her given name was "boring."

Not only that, but "Goldberg" has some validity for her. She has been quoted as saying that she's half-Catholic and half-Jewish and there had been some Goldbergs in her family tree.

Aside from hosting the Oscars, Whoopi Goldberg has also won one herself as Best Supporting Actress for "Ghost" in 1990.

"Dick" Tracy wins Oscar

When Spencer Tracy won his first Best Actor Oscar for "Captains Courageous" in 1937, both he and the Academy were embarrassed.

At the Academy Awards ceremony, Tracy was handed his Oscar. He looked lovingly at it—and then discovered it had been inscribed to Dick Tracy instead of Spencer Tracy.

He got a corrected replacement statue later.

Where to see the best acting off-screen

A comedian once said that if you want to see great acting by movie stars, watch the Academy Awards telecasts.

It was Bob Hope who said, "Keep your eye on the losers, as they smile and applaud the winners. You'll see great understanding, great sportsmanship—and great acting!"

Try this

An amazing number of movies with just one-word titles have won the Oscar for Best Picture. There've been 19 of them through the 2003 awards.

Make a game of seeing how many of the 19 you and your friends can name. Here they are:

1927, "Wings."
1930, "Cimarron."
1932, "Cavalcade."
1940, "Rebecca."
1943, "Casablanca."
1948, "Hamlet."
1955, "Marty."
1958, "Gigi."
1968, "Oliver!"
1970, "Patton."
1976, "Rocky."
1982, "Gandhi."
1984, "Amadeus."
1986, "Platoon."
1992, "Unforgiven."
1995, "Braveheart."
1997, "Titanic."
2000, "Gladiator,"
2002, "Chicago."

SIX

Let The Music Begin

Stories of the musicals,
the singers, the dancers

"You ain't heard nothin' yet"

On the night of Oct. 6, 1927, something new was added to the movies. Warner Brothers premiered "The Jazz Singer" that evening in New York City.

It was the world's first feature-length talkie—and although it goes down in film history as the first "talkie," it was also the movies' first musical feature.

In "The Jazz Singer," after Al Jolson sings a song called "Dirty Hands, Dirty Face," the on-screen audience applauds and Jolson ad-libs, saying, "Wait a minute, folks. Wait a minute. You ain't heard nothin' yet."

Those were the first words ever spoken in a movie. (How true those words were).

"The Jazz Singer" effectively ended the silent era, and the movie was so popular that Hollywood rushed to make, not only more talkies, but more musicals as well.

Of all the countries in the word that make movies, none has come close to America in producing the great quantity and quality of musical films.

Jolson was the third choice

Oddly enough, although the first talkie and musical picture, "The Jazz Singer", was virtually the story of Al Jolson's life (it's about a cantor's son who runs away to become a vaudeville star), and although Jolson himself was a top star, he wasn't the first choice for the movie.

The Warner Brothers offered it first to George Jessel, but he and the Warners couldn't agree on money.

Then they went to Eddie Cantor, but he turned it down.

Finally, they asked Jolson. He agreed, and made movie history.

What was the greatest musical scene?

Choosing the greatest movie musical scene of all time is a matter of opinion and debate.

You might want to pick any of the Busby Berkeley extravagances with creative shots of seemingly hundreds of chorus girls in all sorts of formations, or Judy Garland singing "Over the Rainbow," or Fred and Ginger dancing, or the Pullman car in "42nd Street" full of singers "Shufflin' off to Buffalo," or other memorable and enjoyable numbers, but, the envelope, please for our vote:

We, and many critics, choose Gene Kelly singing, dancing and splashing through the title tune of "Singin' in the Rain" in 1952. Kelly's total exuberance as he swings from a lamppost, jumps on and off curbs, dances through the water and twirls his umbrella creates a classic memory.

Oddly enough, Kelly was ill with a fever when he did that scene.

Not to be forgotten in this movie is the underrated Donald O'Connor's athletic "Make 'em Laugh" number that he ends by crashing though a wall. That scene is a highlight in itself, although it has been overpowered in memory by Kelly's performance.

123

Traditional Christmas song came from a movie

The first time "White Christmas" was ever heard publicly was in the 1942 movie, "Holiday Inn," starring Bing Crosby and Fred Astaire.

In that movie, Irving Berlin songs were used as different holidays took place. For instance, there was "Be Careful It's My Heart" for Valentine's Day," "Easter Parade" for Easter, and so on. Some were old Berlin tunes, but he wrote "White Christmas" especially for this film, and Crosby's rendition became a Christmas standard.

You can win a trivia question by asking what movie introduced "White Christmas," because there was a later film (1954) named "White Christmas," but the song was first heard in "Holiday Inn" 12 years earlier.

"Holiday Inn" is famous for another reason. It was a favorite movie of Kemmons Wilson of Memphis, Tenn. When he started his motel chain after World War II, he named his motels, Holiday Inns.

Surprisingly, Liza won & Judy didn't

Alhough Judy Garland was a long-time, beloved star in movie musicals, she never won a Best Actress Oscar—but her daughter, Liza Minnelli, who had a much shorter film career, did.

Judy rocketed to super-stardom at age 16 when she sang "Over the Rainbow" in "The Wizard of Oz," then starred in such popular musicals as "For Me and My Gal," "Meet Me in St. Louis," "Easter Parade," "In the Good Old Summertime," and her last film, "I Could Go On Singing."

Judy not only lost out on winning any Best Actress Oscars, but also lost the battle of a serene life off-screen. Years of drug and alcohol abuse, and several suicide attempts ended with her death from a drug overdose at age 47.

Among her five husbands was the director of her "Meet Me in St. Louis" film, Vincente Minnelli. Their daughter Liza has had an on-again, off-again show business career that included the movie musical "Cabaret." Liza won the Best Actress Oscar for that picture in 1972.

The movies' most
innovative dance

Fred Astaire dazzled audiences with his classy dancing in over 30 years' worth of films—but perhaps his most spectacular feat was when he danced up the walls—and on the ceiling—in a 1951 movie.

It was in "Royal Wedding," co-starring Jane Powell.

In the film, Fred and Jane are in London for the royal wedding of Princess Elizabeth and Prince Philip.

Fred tells his sister Jane that he'll never fall in love, but if he does she'll know it when he dances on the ceiling

Of course Fred does falls in love. Stanley Donen, who directed so many great musicals, including "Singin' in the Rain," has Astaire start a routine on the floor of his room. But with trick photography, Astaire starts dancing up and down the walls—and then upside down on the ceiling, in one of the best dance numbers of all time.

How did she ever dance?

One of the most unusual Hollywood stars was Carmen Miranda—the "Brazilian Bombshell."

She sang and danced in 14 U.S. movies from 1939 to 1953 with a trademark costume that made you wonder how she could ever dance.

She wore a tall basket full of fruit on her head and 3-inch platform shoes on her feet—but that never seemed to inhibit her ability for frantic dance numbers.

The idea for the fruit basket on her head came from the fact that her father was a wholesale fruit merchant in Brazil.

Her outrageous dances often stole the show from co-stars like Betty Grable, Don Ameche, Alice Faye and even, in one film ("Copacabana"), Groucho Marx.

One critic said, "Despite her ridiculous appearance (or perhaps because of it), she won legions of fans."

Miranda's career and life came to an early end. She died of peritonitis at age 44.

The quick rise & fall
of a great "singer"

A little-known, "B" picture actor, Larry Parks, was chosen to play an all-time great entertainer, Al Jolson, for the 1946 movie "The Jolson Story."

The movie was a surprise hit and Parks achieved sudden fame.

Parks did a great job impersonating Jolson's unique moves when he sang, and was convincing in lip-syncing Jolson's actual voice.

The sequel, "Jolson Sings Again," released in 1949, was not quite the hit the original was, but Parks got continued good reviews.

However, Parks' career plunged as quickly as it had risen. In the early 1950s, he admitted to former membership in the Communist party at the House Un-American Activities Committee hearings on Hollywood.

That was it for Parks as a movie star. Columbia Pictures terminated his contract, and except for a few bit parts for other studios, he never appeared on the screen again.

Parks' wife, Betty Garrett, appeared in some MGM musicals. She later played Archie Bunker's neighbor in TV's "All in the Family."

What Ginger & Fred gave each other

In some of the most elegant romantic musical films ever made, Fred Astaire and Ginger Rogers danced together in a succession of urbane romances, featuring rapturous routines.

Katharine Hepburn once described what Fred and Ginger gave each other. Hepburn said, "He gives her class—and she gives him sex appeal."

Astaire and Rogers' first movie together was "Flying Down to Rio" in 1933 when Ginger was 22 and Astaire, 34. They introduced a dance called "The Carioca" that stole the show.

Over the next six years they were teamed in eight more films: "The Gay Divorcee," "Roberta," "Top Hat" (where they danced to the great song "Cheek to Cheek"), "Follow the Fleet," "Swing Time," "Shall We Dance," "Carefree" and "The Story of Vernon and Irene Castle."

They were never bosom buddies off the screen. As Rogers once said, "We were different people with different interests. We were a couple only on the screen." But they brought a never-to-be-forgotten magic together on the screen.

Astaire's favorite dancing partner was not Ginger Rogers

In a surprising revelation, Fred Astaire said in his autobiography that his favorite dancing partner was not Ginger Rogers—but Rita Hayworth.

Hayworth, perhaps better remembered for her beauty as a movie star than her dancing, was in two films with Astaire, "You'll Never Get Rich" in 1941 and "You Were Never Lovelier" in 1942.

The New York Times once described her as "The epitome of Hollywood glamour and allure, a stunningly beautiful actress." Hayworth was a favorite pinup of GIs in World War II.

But her underrated dancing ability came naturally. Her father, Eduardo Cansino was a Spanish-born dancer and her mother had been a Ziegfeld Follies showgirl. She was born Margarita Cansino. She took her movie name from the Rita of Margarita, and Hayworth from a variation of her mother's maiden name, Haworth.

She appeared in more than 40 films with such co-stars as Spencer Tracy, Cary Grant, Gene Kelly and James Cagney—but perhaps her most famous role was as a temptress in "Gilda" in 1946 when she did what was called a striptease. The "striptease" was limited to removing her arm-length gloves (in a seductive way). The scene became controversial in those days with much criticism from some people.

Hayworth was married five times. Among her husbands were Orson Welles, Dick Haymes and Prince Aly Khan, the son of the spiritual leader of millions of Ismaili Muslims.

She spent her last years incapacitated with Alzheimer's disease, and cared for by Princess Yasmin Aga Khan, her daughter with Prince Aly Khan.

Another surprise about Rita and Ginger

Not only is it surprising to learn that Fred Astaire chose Rita Hayworth over Ginger Rogers as his favorite dancing partner, but here's another fact that is little known. Rita and Ginger were closer than you may have thought.

These rival superstars were first cousins.

Their mothers were sisters.

SEVEN

What they didn't want you to see & hear

The stories of Hollywood's
censorship

What you weren't allowed to see or hear in Hollywood movies

It's difficult to realize now what could NOT be shown or spoken in mainstream American movies of the 1930s and '40s—Hollywood's so-called Golden Years—when so many all-time, popular film classics were made.

Tough censorship rules, known as the Production Code, were in effect then.

The code not only prohibited any four-letter "vulgar and profane expressions," but also banned the use of the words God, Lord, Jesus and Christ, unless, as the code said, "they were used reverently." Also banned were these specific words: hell, damn and S.O.B.

The code said, "no movie shall be made that shows excessive or lustful kissing, lustful embracing, suggestive postures or gestures, and illegal drug traffic."

Further: "Indecent or undue exposure is forbidden.

"Seduction or rape should never be more than suggested, and they are never the proper subject for comedy.

Censorship

"Sex perversion or any inference to it is forbidden.

"Sex hygiene and venereal diseases are not subjects for motion pictures.

"Sex relationships between the white and black races is forbidden.

"The sanctity of marriage and the home shall be upheld.

"Methods of crime shall not be explicitly presented.

"Ministers of religion shall not be used as comic characters or villains, and no film may throw ridicule on any religious faith.

"Pictures shall not be produced which will lower the standards of those who see it. The sympathy of the audience should never be thrown to the side of crime, wrongdoing, evil or sin."

Even though it wasn't mentioned specifically in the code, most producers went so far as to always show twin beds, and not a double bed, in bedrooms, to make sure their films were as "clean" as possible.

The beginning of
the end of
the code

The Production Code was not mandated by the government—but it was the movie industry's own list of censorship rules that executives felt would keep the government and religious groups away from their doors.

After World War II, the code slowly began to break down. Some producers began to test it, but the real forces to abolish the code gradually came from a combination of social change in the nation, Supreme Court decisions on free speech, civil liberties groups, and the influence of racy foreign films that began to draw larger audiences in America.

Eventually, a rating system for movies was put into place, supposedly to protect children, and in any event, the old code would be gone.

How "damn" slipped into "Gone With the Wind"

The Production Code, as we mentioned, banned the use of words like "damn" in movies made in the 1930s.

But producer David O. Selznick was determined to fight the code for one particular movie, "Gone With the Wind" in 1939, and allow Clark Gable to utter the famous line from the book, "Frankly my dear, I don't give a damn."

Selznick pleaded his case to the code office and to the public. He said that millions of people had already read the book, and Selznick felt it was an essential line in the story.

After much hemming and hawing by the code people, Selznick had a deal. He was told he could use the line if he paid a fine of $5,000. Selznick glady obliged and movie history was made.

Still, some of the public in those days were shocked to hear that obscenity, as mild as it was, on the screen. Amazingly, it created somewhat of a sensation around the country.

Howard Hughes was another producer who started cracking the code. He had made what some called a sexy western, "The Outlaw," starring Jane Russell. Hughes fought with the code people for three years to allow the movie to be released. His battle got so much publicity that when he did offer it to theaters in 1946, many gladly took it, knowing it would do great business. Moviegoers lined up in big numbers to see it.

It turned out that the movie wasn't very good, and a lot of people wondered what all the fuss was about.

Perhaps the most significant movie that eventually began to break the code was "The Moon is Blue" in 1953. It dealt with the issue of virginity—a code no-no. Again, all the publicity generated by producer Otto Preminger turned into big box office when Preminger got the film into some theaters. Other producers began to realize that the code had become outdated. And slowly, the code began to crumble.

Preminger drove one of the last nails into the coffin of the code in 1955 when he went ahead with "The Man With the Golden Arm," a story about drug addiction, heretofore taboo.

Times were changing, and the code died soon after.

What those
ratings mean

After the breakup of Hollywood's tough Production Code censorship rules, filmmakers were free to show almost anything they wanted, and have actors say just about any profanity that exists in the world today.

Ratings were established for each movie in 1968. "G" stood for General Audiences and meant that all ages were admitted. "M" stood for Mature Audiences (all ages admitted, but parental guidance was suggested). "R" was Restricted (children under 16 not admitted without a parent or guardian). "X" meant no one under 17 admitted.

The ratings were modified in years following. "M" was changed to "PG," later split into "PG" and "PG-13" (Parents strongly cautioned. Some material may be inappropriate for pre-teenagers). "X" was changed to "NC-17."

Meantime, makers of porno films capitalized on the rating system, using their own unofficial designations of XX or XXX or XXXX. Everybody got the idea.

How an actress
beat the censors

In the era when Hollywood censorship of sex was at its toughest, one actress beat the system.

In 1935, Mae West was the highest paid woman in America as a result of her movie and stage stardom—and that stardom throughout the '30s was built on her sexual innuendoes.

How did she get away with it?

West, who wrote her own lines for her movies, used double entendres that poked fun at sex. She never used forbidden 4-letter words or really did anything the censors could stop—but the meaning of her lines was clear.

In one movie, another woman admires her jewelry by saying, "Goodness, what beautiful diamonds." West replied, "Goodness had nothing to do with it, honey."

In another film she said, "I used to be Snow White but I drifted." Other lines included, "Men I don't like don't exist," "It's better to be looked over than overlooked," and her trademark, "Come up and see me sometime."

(She actually said, "Come up sometime and see me," to Cary Grant in the movie "Diamond Lil," but the line has been misquoted so often that people don't remember the exact original. Language expert William Safire says the remembered version is more rhythmical and sexier, and even Bartlett's Quotations lists "Come up and see me sometime" attributed to West).

Mae also displayed her full bosom proudly, and during World War II, sailors and airmen named their inflatable life jackets "Mae Wests," a name still used today.

Among her movies were "She Done Him Wrong," "I'm No Angel," "Night After Night," "Goin' To Town," "Diamond Lil," "Go West Young Man" and "My Little Chickadee."

West was still going strong at age 78 in 1970, when she played in "Myra Breckinridge," and at age 86 when she was in "Sextette."

EIGHT

Behind The Scenes

The original Fox,
and other stories
of the directors,
producers and studios

The original Fox

The Fox movie studio which begot today's Fox television, including Fox News, Fox Sports, etc., was started by a man named Fox—except that wasn't his real name.

William Fox, as he was known in Hollywood's heyday, was born Wilhelm Fried in Hungary. He came to America, changed his name to Fox, and founded one of the major movie companies.

He was one of many first-or-second-generation Jewish immigrants who headed the big film studios in the golden era of the 1930s. Others were Louis B. Mayer at MGM; Harry, Sam, Albert and Jack Warner at Warner Brothers; Harry Cohn at Columbia; Carl Laemmle at Universal; Adolph Zukor at Paramount and Samuel Goldwyn at Goldwyn Pictures.

Long after Fox's death, newspaper and TV magnate Rupert Murdoch bought the company in the 1980s and split it into Fox movies and Fox television.

So the name of William Fox, nee Wilhelm Fried, lives on.

The Boy Wonder
& Last Tycoon

One of the most interesting people in Hollywood history was Irving G. Thalberg.

Amazingly, this young, sickly man became a powerful studio executive at age 20 at Universal, then at age 25, at MGM, where he was head of production, and responsible for all that studio's movies.

Called "The Boy Wonder," Thalberg had an uncanny ability to pick the right stars and stories, and helped make MGM a top studio.

As a child he had been stricken with rheumatic fever that damaged his heart. He was told he might not live past his 30s. Knowing he might have a short life and career, he worked long feverish hours when he got to Hollywood.

He was such a perfectionist that he had scenes re-shot many times. He often said, "Movies aren't made, they're remade."

Thalberg married a glamorous movie star, Norma Shearer, and helped give her the identity of "The First Lady of the Screen."

In his 30s, he suffered a heart attack. He took some time off, but then returned to work to produce what would be his last film. It was the award-winning "The Good Earth." He died shortly after, at age 37, in 1936.

This young giant of the movie industry is honored today with the well-known Irving G. Thalberg Award. It's given at the Academy Awards for "long-term outstanding motion picture production." It's presented only in years when academy officials feel there's a worthy recipient.

F. Scott Fitzgerald wrote a book based on Thalberg's life, and he called it "The Last Tycoon."

It was made into a movie in 1976 with Robert DeNiro playing the Thalberg role.

Boy wonder, No. 2

Much like Irving G. Thalberg who became a production force in Hollywood beginning at age 20, Steven Spielberg also became a Boy Wonder in movieland.

Spielberg started making movies at home in Arizona when he was 12 years old. He made a little 3-minute home western then, and as a teenager continued to make his own more-and-more ambitious films. By the time he was 21, he sold a short to Universal. They were so impressed with his work that they gave him a 7-year contract. He was on his way.

At age 23 he directed the acclaimed "Duel" and then "The Sugarland Express."

His major breakthrough came when he was 28 and filmed his first blockbuster, "Jaws."

At age 30, he directed "Close Encounters of the Third Kind" and the hits continued.

He's directed and/or produced such other famous movies as "E.T." "Indiana Jones," "Jurassic Park," "Raiders of the Lost Ark," "Saving Private Ryan" and "Schindler's List."

Born in 1947, Spielberg can no longer be called a Boy Wonder, but he earned that title in his youth.

Same family brought you James Bond—and broccoli

A man named Albert Broccoli brought the popular James Bond series to the screen, producing the original Bond movies.

And, yes, the vegetable broccoli was named for this man's family.

Albert Broccoli, the film producer, is a descendant of a prominent Italian farm family that created broccoli. They modified cauliflower to produce broccoli—and named it after themselves.

Only one man ever had this thrill

John Huston directed many great films—but two of them gave him a special joy.

He directed his father, Walter, to an Oscar for Best Supporting Actor in "The Treasure of the Sierra Madre"—and he directed his daughter, Anjelica, to an Oscar for Best Supporting Actress in "Prizzi's Honor."

John himself won the Oscar for Best Director for "Sierra Madre," making the Huston family the first in Hollywood history to have three generations honored by the Academy.

Who were
Metro, Goldwyn and Mayer?

Perhaps the most famous American movie studio of all time was Metro-Goldwyn-Mayer, or MGM.

They used to advertise, with some exaggeration, that they had "more stars than there are in the heavens."

Despite the exaggeration, they did have many of the most popular stars in Hollywood in the days when actors and actresses were under contract to their studios. The MGM movies of their glory years from the 1920s to the '50s, featured Clark Gable, Judy Garland, Greta Garbo, Joan Crawford, Spencer Tracy, Robert Taylor, Mickey Rooney, Gene Kelly and Elizabeth Taylor, among many others.

The company was founded in 1924 with a merger among the Metro Picture Corporation, Samuel Goldwyn Pictures and Louis B. Mayer Pictures.

It's odd to note that Goldwyn left the company soon after it was formed, and wasn't around when all the big MGM hits were made—but his name remained in the corporate title of Metro-Goldwyn-Mayer.

Immortal Goldwynisms

Samuel Goldwyn, a successful independent Hollywood producer for over 50 years, lives on in legend not only for his movies but also for his malapropisms.

Goldwyn was born in Poland and came to the U.S. with the name Samuel Goldfish.

He married Blanche Lasky, a sister of vaudeville producer Jesse Lasky who introduced Goldfish to show business.

They went into the movie-making business, and after making some films with Lasky, Goldfish formed his own movie company with a man named Edgar Selwyn. They called it the Goldwyn Co., taking the "Gold" from Goldfish's name and the "wyn" from Selwyn. Goldfish liked the company name so much, he adopted it as his own name. He then went to MGM, left there, and began a string of his own hit movies—and Goldwynisms. His famous quotes:

"Include me out."

"A verbal contract isn't worth the paper it's written on."

"In two words: im-possible."

"Anybody who sees a psychiatrist should have their head examined."

151

The terrible life
of 2003 Oscar winner

Roman Polanski, who won the Best Director Oscar for "The Pianist" in 2003, had more than one lifetime of tragedies and troubles.

When he was a child of 8 in his native Poland, his parents were sent to concentration camps during World War II. Polanski was left to fend for himself, living alone on the streets.

He found solace from his awful existence by watching as many movies as he could. As a teenager he became an actor and then entered the Polish Film School where he made some award-winning short films.

Paramount Pictures brought him to Hollywood where he made a successful horror movie, "Rosemary's Baby." He married Sharon Tate, but tragedy struck again. Tate was savagely murdered by the Charles Manson gang.

After trying to recover from that gruesome event, Polanski directed one of his best films, "Chinatown," but then was arrested for allegedly raping a 13-year-old girl. He fled to Europe where he's made some more successful movies, including "Tess," and the Academy Award-winning "The Pianist."

Downgrading a classic

According to many movie experts, the first important film classic made in America was D.W. Griffith's "The Birth of a Nation" (1915).

It revolutionized filmmaking with moveable cameras, sophisticated editing and epic panoramas.

David Wark Griffith, who co-wrote and directed the movie, was a Southerner, and he told the story of the Civil War and its aftermath from a Southern point of view.

While the film has been praised for its production values, it has been called racist. The last scene is especially distasteful to many as the Ku Klux Klan rides to rescue two women held by a black man.

Griffith was so embarrassed by the criticism he got for the story, that he followed it with a film that explored the evils of hatred, called "Intolerance."

Griffith went on to make other movies into the 1930s, but the main place he holds in film history is with his role of production genius on one hand, and vilified storyteller on the other, for his landmark "Birth of a Nation."

153

Disney did NOT
draw or name
Mickey Mouse

Although Walt Disney is forever linked with Mickey Mouse, there are several surprising facts about Disney's involvement.

It turns out that Disney, despite his role in creating animation in movies, was a less than good artist himself. He's been described as average at best—and he could never make a good drawing of Mickey.

That job went to a Disney assistant, Ub Iwerks, who drew Mickey most of time in the beginning years. Disney did do Mickey's voice in many shorts and longer films.

Mickey Mouse made his debut in a short called "Steamboat Willie" in 1928. But Disney had a different name for him. He originally was going to call him Mortimer Mouse.

Disney's wife Lillian told her husband that name was too formal—and it was Lillian who suggested the name Mickey.

154

Quiz on directors

1. Who holds the record for winning an Oscar for Best Director the most times (through 2003)?

2. What man directed both "Gone With the Wind" and "The Wizard of Oz" the same year?

3. Oddly, six of the first eight Oscars for Best Director went to men named Frank. Can you name them?

(Answers)

1. John Ford for "The Informer," "The Grapes of Wrath," "How Green Was My Valley" and "The Quiet Man."

2. Victor Fleming.

3. Frank Borzage twice, Frank Lloyd twice, Frank Capra twice.

155

NINE

Film Clips

Why movies are called flicks,
And other "did you knows"

Did you know...

- Why are movies called flicks? Years ago, people called movies flickers because of the flickering of light from the projector. Gradually the word flickers was shortened to flicks—and the term is still used today.

- The Top Dog in Hollywood was literally a dog in 1926. In a poll of favorite movie stars that year, the dog Rin Tin Tin finished first.

- In what movie did Clint Eastwood first utter his famous line, "Make my day?" It was in "Sudden Impact" in 1983.

- "Doctor Zhivago," which supposedly had sweeping scenes of Russia, was actually filmed in Finland. The musical "Oklahoma" was filmed in Arizona because the director thought Arizona looked more like Oklahoma than Oklahoma did. The real Casablanca is in Africa, but the movie "Casablanca" was filmed in Van Nuys, Calif.

Did you know...

- In his various movies, Humphrey Bogart was shot 12 times, electrocuted or hanged 8 times and jailed 9 times.

- The great director Alfred Hitchcock never won an Oscar for Best Director.

- What movie had the most songs in it? It was the 1946 "Jolson Story." Al Jolson (lip- synced by Larry Parks) sang 28 different songs.

- Among Elizabeth Taylor's many off-screen, real-life husbands have been actor Richard Burton (twice), singer Eddie Fisher, Hilton Hotel heir Nicky Hilton, actor Michael Wilding, showman Mike Todd, and U.S. Senator John Warner.

- In what movie did Shirley Temple sing her famous song, "On the Good Ship Lollypop"? The answer is "Bright Eyes," which she made when she was 6 years old.

Did you know...

- "It's a Wonderful Life" with Jimmy Stewart is now a beloved classic—but it was panned and did disappointing business when it was first released in 1946.

- Hollywood got its name when a Mrs. Horace Wilcox moved to undeveloped Southern California in 1887. She planted some holly bushes and called the area "Hollywood."

- Betty Hutton, the vivacious, popular star of big musicals like "Annie Get Your Gun" and "The Greatest Show on Earth," suffered from personal and financial problems a few years after making her last movie. Eventually she was discovered working as a cleaning lady in Rhode Island.

- Oddly, Mario Lanza, who played Enrico Caruso in "The Great Caruso," was born on the very day that Caruso died in 1921.

Did you know...

- A theater in Manteca, Calif., was showing "The Towering Inferno." One night during the run, the theater caught fire and became a towering inferno. Likewise, a Pittsburgh theater had a fire the night it began showing "Too Hot to Handle."

- Only once in Academy Awards history have a movie AND its sequel both won Best Picture Oscars: "The Godfather" won in 1972 and "Godfather Part II" won in 1974.

- How many "Andy Hardy" films were made? There were 15 of them, between 1937 and 1947.

- Ads for the 1956 movie "Baby Doll" proudly carried the line that the movie was condemned by Cardinal Spellman. Producers thought that would help box office sales.

- The copyright dates of most movies are listed on the screen in Roman numerals to keep people from quickly figuring out how old the movie is.

Cowboy trivia:
What were their horses' names?

Gene Autry (whose real first name was Orvon) was not the first singing cowboy in the movies, but he was, by far, the most successful.

His first film was "Tumbling Tumbleweeds" in 1933—and he went on from there to make the incredible number of 93 movies.

His horse's name? Answer: Champion.

Autry was succeeded as "The King of the Cowboys" by Roy Rogers (whose real name was Leonard Slye).

Rogers made 34 movies and then took his act to TV for the long-running "Roy Rogers Show," with his wife, Dale Evans.

Rogers' horse? It was Trigger.

Trigger was billed as "the smartest horse in the movies." When the horse died, Rogers had him stuffed and put on display.

Unlike many Hollywood stars who squandered their money, both Autry and Rogers wound up as extremely wealthy men. Autry bought radio and TV stations and owned the California Angels baseball team. Rogers made big money by owning his TV series.

She was a he

What would an aspiring actor or actress give to became a star in the movies—and have his or her name in the title of a series of films.

One who did all those things wasn't a human, but a dog named Lassie.

The first Lassie movie was "Lassie Come Home" in 1943. (11-year-old Elizabeth Taylor was in that film, and they both did pretty well after that.)

"Lassie Come Home" was so popular that additional Lassie movies were planned. Six more were made between 1945 and 1951. After that came a popular, long-running Lassie television series. Lassie TV shows can still be seen in syndication.

But there are several things about Lassie that weren't quite what they seemed.

Over the long period of time that the movies and TV shows were made, there was obviously more than one Lassie. At least six different collies were used to play Lassie.

Then, there's the fact that Lassie was always referred to as "she." But every dog who played Lassie was a male. Dog experts say that while female collies are smarter, male collies are usually better looking.

One last note about Lassie: When the first movie was planned, the film studio had screen tests for the part, just as they do for human actors. More than 300 collies showed up for the audition. A collie named Pal won the audition, and his name was quickly changed to Lassie.

Tough guy
on baby food

Humphrey Bogart, who had a tough guy image in many films, was a model when he was a child in New York City.

One of his modeling jobs was posing for a picture on Gerber baby food jars.

"Who's on First?"
came from a movie

A movie scene became a classic comedy routine when Bud Abbott and Lou Costello did their now-famous "Who's on First?" baseball skit in a 1945 film.

It was in "The Naughty Nineties," an otherwise forgettable movie where Bud and Lou find themselves with Mississippi riverboat gamblers.

Costello asks Abbott, "Who's on first?" Abbott tries to explain that Who is the first baseman's name, and keeps saying, "Who's on first." Costello says, "That's what I'm asking, who's on first?" Abbott says, "That's right, Who's on first." Costello gets more and more frustrated and it goes from there with names like What's on second and I Don't Know on third.

Abbott and Costello performed their movie routine for years afterward on radio, TV and in personal appearances. A copy of it is in baseball's Hall of Fame in Cooperstown, N.Y.

166

Marilyn Monroe's famous photo

Before she became a superstar in the movies, Marilyn Monroe posed for a nude calendar photo.

She was paid just $50.

After she became famous, it's been reported that more than one million of those photos have been sold.

The Charlie Chan oddity

Among the most popular detective movies of all time were the Charlie Chan films.

Hollywood made 43 Chan movies about the wise Chinese detective, and three different actors played Chan over the years—but none was Chinese.

Chan was played by Warner Oland, Sidney Toler and Roland Winters.

TEN

Movie Biz

The food that saved theaters
and other stories

The food that
saved movie theaters

Oddly, there's one kind of food that has often kept theaters in business.

Beginning in the 1930s, theater owners discovered that moviegoers love to eat popcorn when watching a film. Almost every theater in the country started selling popcorn—and because of the economics of the film industry, there were, and are, many days when theaters make more money from popcorn than they do from the movies themselves.

Theater owners usually only get a percentage of the money people pay for tickets. There are many different deals, but of all the money taken in at the box office, a major percentage often goes to the company that made the film, leaving the individual theater with a smaller slice of the gross.

Such is not the case with popcorn. It can be bought cheaply, marked up nicely, and combined with soft drinks and candy. All that money belongs to the theater—and is often the difference between profit and loss.

Spying outside
the theater

In the early days of movies when film companies began to rent their films to theaters on a percentage basis, a typical deal was 40% of ticket sales to the theater, and 60% to the film company —but how would the film company know if the theater was giving them an honest count of people paying to see the movie?

The custom began of having "checkers" sitting in a car or standing near a theater, checking the number of moviegoers going to the box office. This cloak and dagger stuff worked two ways though.

Theater owners became aware of the checkers, who were often low-paid. Some owners figured out that they could slip the checker a few bucks to fudge his counts.

Then the film companies struck back. They hired other checkers to check on their original checkers. So there were checkers—and checkers on the checkers — outside theaters.

Today, of course, most theaters are computerized. The old checkers are just a funny memory.

The first movie

Moving pictures had been developed earlier, but the first real movie—the first with a plot—was "The Great Train Robbery," in 1903.

It featured the first cowboy star, Broncho Billy Anderson.

Lasting 12 minutes, it told the story of villains sneaking on a train, robbing it, then being chased by a posse until they are gunned down—a basic plot that would be repeated one way or another hundreds of times in future movies.

They cut to the chase early in this one.

It cost a nickel
to see a movie

The first movie theater in America was in downtown Pittsburgh in 1905.

There had been other places in other cities that showed movies from time-to-time, but the Pittsburgh location was the first devoted exclusively to motion pictures on a daily basis.

The theater was called the Nickelodeon because it cost a nickel to get in and watch a movie. That became a popular name, and Nickelodeons sprung up across the country.

The movie
was secondary

The world's first drive-in movie theater opened in Camden, N.J., in June of 1933.

Soon, drive-ins began appearing elsewhere—and they proved to be particularly popular with couples on dates.

The owner of one drive-in said he never bothered to put the current movie's name on the marquee because it didn't matter what was playing to many dating couples.

There were over 6,000 drive-ins in America at their peak in the early 1950s. But the number began to diminish with the advent of television and the realization that the drive-ins' property could be more valuable when used for such things as the growing need for shopping centers and other suburban developments.

The biggest drive-in ever built, by the way, was in Lynn, Mass. It had room for 5,000 cars. Assuming a minimum of two occupants per car, that was a potential audience of at least 10,000—far exceeding any indoor movie theater in the world.

"Television will
never last"—movie man says

Hollywood was terrified when TV sets started appearing in homes across America after World War II. Some predicted the end of the movie business. "Experts" said people will stay home and not go out to movie theaters anymore.

Producer Darryl Zanuck tried to counter the panic in Hollywood. He said, in a famous quote, "Television will never last because people will soon get tired of staring at a box every night."

It turned out, of course, that both the experts and Zanuck were wrong. Although movie attendance did suffer in the early years of TV, the industry survived and has bigger box office receipts today than ever imagined in the 1940s.

The movie industry also profited from a wedding of sorts with TV. Studios were kept busy making shows for television, and film companies sold their old films to TV at nice prices.

Theaters changed radically, too, with today's big, multi-screen complexes generally replacing the old, single-screen buildings.

The movies and TV both made it.

The scandals
of Hollywood

Swedish-born Ingrid Bergman was one of the most popular movie stars in America in the 1940s. Fans loved her performance in "Casablanca" and other films.

But in 1949 she left her husband, Dr. Peter Lindstrom, and daughter Pia (who would later become a TV personality). Ingrid flew off to Italy to be with director Roberto Rossellini. Soon, word came that she had a child with Rossellini.

It was a national scandal in the U.S. She was denounced on the floor of Congress as Hollywood's "apostle of degradation." Added to the irony was that Bergman had been seen as so pure and wholesome and had recently played a nun in "Bells of St. Mary's," and a saint in "Joan of Arc."

She made five films with Rossellini, but they were largely boycotted in America. Her name was mud. Clergymen urged parishioners not to patronize her pictures.

Amazingly, as bad as Bergman's image was at the time, she made a spectacular comeback. Changing social mores had something to do with it, and her on-screen persona helped.

20th Century-Fox took a chance with Bergman and hired her to star in "Anastasia" in 1956. The film was a hit and Bergman won the Best Actress Oscar (showing that the Academy Awards held no grudges).

The first great scandal in Hollywood involved one of the most popular early comedy actors, Fatty Arbuckle. Fans loved him until he was accused of rape and manslaughter in the death of a woman named, oddly enough, Virginia Rappe. Although Arbuckle was later acquitted on all counts, he was never accepted again as a funny man on the screen. Arbuckle's career was finished.

Many other Hollywood stars involved in reported sexual adventures got by with a wink and a smile from their fans. The swashbuckling Errrol Flynn, for instance, had his name enter in the language with the so-called humorous expression, "in like Flynn," after he was accused and acquitted of statutory rape.

Outside of Arbuckle, film careers have generally not been ruined by behavior that might topple other public figures. Stars like Elizabeth Taylor, Charlie Chaplin, Jane Fonda and Marilyn Monroe survived, and in the case of Monroe, her posing nude for a calendar, and alleged affairs with high officials, helped her career.

The most famous headline
about the movies

On July 17, 1935, the show business newspaper, Variety, ran a headline that's become a classic.

The headline said, "Sticks Nix Hick Pix."

Variety had a special lingo all its own, coining such words as boffo and socko (for good), pix (for movies), legit (for Broadway plays), biz (for business), B.O. (for box office) and cuffo (from "on the cuff" or free).

Their famous headline meant that people in rural areas—the Sticks—(or as Variety also wrote in the story, "The Silo Belt") were becoming more sophisticated and were rejecting (Nix) corny (Hick) movies (Pix). The accompanying story said Hollywood was turning to more mature story material.

Variety has had another classic headline that lives in journalism lore. On Oct. 30, 1929, a day after the infamous stock market crash that ushered in the Great Depression, Variety wrote, "Wall St. Lays An Egg."

Accident creates
Hollywood tradition

Because a movie star accidentally tripped and fell one day, a Hollywood tradition was born.

Actress Norma Talmadge was walking with actor Douglas Fairbanks Jr. in 1927.

She tripped in front of Grauman's Chinese Theater and fell into wet cement.

Her hand and footprints were in the cement—and that created the idea of starting a famous tourist attraction. Since 1927, hundreds of movie stars have put hand and footprints—on purpose—into the cement.

Young girl
beats them all

The youngest person in America ever to earn $1 million on his or her own was a little girl not quite 10 years old.

By the time Shirley Temple was 10, she had earned over $1 million from her series of hit films and endorsements.

And those were 1930s dollars.

ELEVEN

The Top 100

The American Film Institute's
best movies ever made

Best movies
of all time

The American Film Institute polled 1,500 people—most of whom were from the film world, including actors, directors, screenwriters, critics, etc., and asked them to name the 100 best movies ever made.

Two cautionary notes: This poll includes only movies made through 1996. Secondly, the poll was for the best American movies, so you will find no foreign films.

All things considered though, this is a useful guide to keep for all-time movies to see.

Almost all are available on video today, and many are also on DVDs.

The year each film was originally released follows the tile. An asterisk means the movie won the Oscar for Best Picture.

Let's take a look:

Best movies
1-20

1. Citizen Kane, 1941
2. Casablanca, 1942*
3. The Godfather, 1972*
4. Gone with the Wind, 1939*
5. Lawrence of Arabia, 1962*
6. The Wizard of Oz, 1939
7. The Graduate, 1967
8. On the Waterfront, 1954*
9. Schindler's List, 1993*
10. Singin' in the Rain, 1952

11. It's a Wonderful Life, 1946
12. Sunset Boulevard, 1950
13. The Bridge on the River Kwai, 1957*
14. Some Like It Hot, 1959
15. Star Wars, 1977
16. All About Eve, 1950*
17. The African Queen, 1951
18. Psycho, 1960
19. Chinatown, 1974
20. One Flew Over the Cuckoo's Nest, 1975*

Best movies
21-40

21. The Grapes of Wrath, 1940
22. 2001: A Space Odyssey, 1968
23. The Maltese Falcon, 1941
24. Raging Bull, 1980
25. E.T.: The Extra Terrestrial, 1982
26. Dr. Strangelove, 1964
27. Bonnie and Clyde, 1967
28. Apocalypse Now, 1979
29. Mr. Smith Goes to Washington, 1939
30. The Treasure of the Sierra Madre, 1948

31. Annie Hall, 1977*
32. The Godfather Part II, 1974*
33. High Noon, 1952
34. To Kill a Mockingbird, 1962
35. It Happened One Night, 1934*
36. Midnight Cowboy, 1969*
37. The Best Years of Our Lives, 1946*
38. Double Indemnity, 1944
39. Doctor Zhivago, 1965
40. North by Northwest, 1959

Best Movies
41-60

41. West Side Story, 1961*
42. Rear Window, 1954
43. King Kong, 1933
44. The Birth of a Nation, 1915
45. A Streetcar Named Desire, 1951
46. A Clockwork Orange, 1971
47. Taxi Driver, 1976
48. Jaws, 1975
49. Snow White and the Seven Dwarfs, 1937
50. Butch Cassidy and the Sundance Kid, 1969

51. The Philadelphia Story, 1940
52. From Here to Eternity, 1953*
53. Amadeus, 1984*
54. All Quiet on the Western Front, 1930*
55. The Sound of Music, 1965*
56. M*A*S*H, 1970
57. The Third Man, 1949
58. Fantasia, 1940
59. Rebel Without a Cause, 1955
60. Raiders of the Lost Ark, 1981

Best Movies
61-80

61. Vertigo, 1958
62. Tootsie, 1982
63. Stagecoach, 1939
64. Close Encounters of the Third Kind, 1977
65. The Silence of the Lambs, 1991*
66. Network, 1976
67. The Manchurian Candidate, 1962
68. An American in Paris, 1951*
69. Shane, 1953
70. The French Connection, 1971*

71. Forrest Gump, 1994*
72. Ben-Hur, 1959*
73. Wuthering Heights, 1939
74. The Gold Rush, 1925
75. Dances with Wolves, 1990*
76. City Lights, 1931
77. American Graffiti, 1973
78. Rocky, 1976*
79. The Deer Hunter, 1978*
80. The Wild Bunch, 1969

Best Movies
81-100

81. Modern Times, 1936
82. Giant, 1956
83. Platoon, 1986*
84. Fargo, 1996
85. Duck Soup, 1933
86. Mutiny on the Bounty, 1935*
87. Frankenstein, 1931
88. Easy Rider, 1969
89. Patton, 1970*
90. The Jazz Singer, 1927

91. My Fair Lady, 1964*
92. A Place in the Sun, 1951
93. The Apartment, 1960*
94. Goodfellas, 1990
95. Pulp Fiction, 1994
96. The Searchers, 1956
97. Bringing Up Baby, 1938
98. Unforgiven, 1992*
99. Guess Who's Coming to Dinner, 1967
100. Yankee Doodle Dandy, 1942

Order Additional Books as Gifts

Knowledge in a Nutshell on the Movies
(ISBN 0-9660991-2-5)

Quantity_____@ $9.50 each

Total_____

Add $2.50 for shipping & handling for first book and 50 cents for each additional book.

Grand total_____

Discounts available for six or more books.

Call 1-800-NUTSHELL (1-800-688-7435) for information and/or credit card orders, or send check or money order to Knowledge in a Nutshell Inc., 1420 Centre Avenue, Suite 2213, Pittsburgh PA 15219, or visit www.knowledgeinanutshell.com.

Name_____

Address_____

City/State/Zip_____

Other Books in the Series

Knowledge in a Nutshell...Over 500 amazing fun facts and stories...Find out about the one man present when THREE U.S. Presidents were assassinated; which U.S. state no longer exists.

Knowledge in a Nutshell on Sports...The perfect book for sports buffs...Find out about the 6-inch home run; why golf courses have 18 holes; the great football team that never existed.

Knowledge in a Nutshell on Popular Products– Heinz Edition...Fun food facts and stories plus international recipes; why hamburgers are called hamburgers even thought they have no ham; how vinegar can help you around the house.

Knowledge in a Nutshell on America...The amazing story of the real Uncle Sam and his boyhood friend; surprising stories about patriotic songs.

Knowledge in a Nutshell on Success...Thoughts to help you feel better and do better.

Discounts available on the set of books. Call 1-800-NUTSHELL (1-800-688-7435).

The Edible Game A Smart Cookie™

**The perfect food for the hungry mind...
you can't eat just one—you'll want to
know more and eat more**

**There are cookies and there are games—
This gives you both**

America's answer to the fortune cookie, this walnut-shaped cookie has fascinating questions and answers in each one. The only game where you can eat the game board.

The cookies, designed by international architect Slyvester Damianos, FAIA, and baked by Jenny Lee Bakery, a 75-year-old Pittsburgh bakery, are available in a gift box of 12 ($14.95 + s/h), or 20 individually-wrapped cookies in a tub ($24.95 + s/h).

TO ORDER: Call 1-800-NUTSHELL
(1-800-688-7435) or visit
www.knowledgeinanutshell.com.

Bulk orders and custom questions available for special occasions.

Printed in the United States
92136LV00001B/47/A